Making Workgroups Effective

Effective

Fourth Edition

Hedley G. Dimock
and
Raye Kass

Captus Press

Making Workgroups Effective, 4th edition

Captus Press Inc.
Units 14 & 15
1600 Steeles Avenue West
Concord, Ontario
Canada L4K 4M2
Phone: (416) 736-5537
Fax: (416) 736-5793
Email: info@captus.com
Internet: http://www.captus.com

Library and Archives Canada Cataloguing in Publication

Dimock, Hedley G.
    Making workgroups effective / Hedley Dimock and
Rachel Kass. — 4th ed.

(Dimock series on groups)
1st and 2nd eds have title: Factors in working with groups.
Includes bibliographical references
ISBN 978-1-55322-236-1

    1. Social groups. 2. Terms in the workplace. 3. Leadership.
4. Group relations training. 5. Virtual work teams. I. Kass,
Rachel R. II. Title. III. Series: Dimock series on groups

HM131.D54 2011   302.3   2011-905133-8

Canada ▮◆▮ *We acknowledge the financial support of the
Government of Canada through the Canada
Book Fund for our publishing activities.*

0 9 8 7 6 5 4 3 2 1
Printed in Canada

Contents

Contents

Preface

It was clear to me [Hedley], when I started writing this edition that the impact of the digital revolution was going to be a major focus of it. But I did not realize the speed of the technological changes and their impact on group behaviour would have me feeling I was on a virtual treadmill trying to keep up with them.

When I started this book many months ago, for example, I believed that the virtual groups of the Internet would not have the strong commitment to collaborate work as face groups and thus not be as effective in accomplishing tasks. However, the successful use of the Internet in early 2011 facilitated the demise of the long-term dictators in Egypt and Tunisia. The Canadian CRTC recently made an anti-consumer change in Internet charges and a huge electronically generated petition pushed the governing politicians to cancel it. So the power is definitely there to accomplish tasks more effectively than I believed.

The changes erupting from the digital revolution have led to major paradigm shifts in our society, especially in the role and function of the groups within it. Consequently, this book has more additions and changes than any of the score and a half I have previously produced. Over half of this fourth edition is new material, much of it written by Raye Kass. I find it a bit ironic to have produced a longer printed book when the trend is toward electronic media and our readers are expecting shorter presentations with more immediate satisfaction.

Twitter is limited to 140 characters and can get you an immediate response, ads on TV may last 15 seconds, and stocks that people held for an average of over eight years now average nine months, pushing the stock to seek immediate returns. Another result of this "me-now" drive has been to push Canada's personal debt load to 145 percent, the highest of any developed country. The impacts of these shifts on the new reality groups of the digital generation are twofold. First, attention spans can be quite short and planning for results a short time frame.

This tends to short-change team-building activity such as interpersonal awareness and trust development. Members' comfort and commitment suffer here as well as group solidarity. Secondly, in the haste for immediate results, the group may shortcut the logical steps in collaborate decision making and use quick votes instead. This "no short-term pain for long-term gain" approach weakens the quality of group decisions and the satisfaction of members with them.

The jury is still out on some of the social/cultural changes resulting from the digital revolution. A study reported in 2011 found that 62 percent of youth's discretionary time was spent as individuals using their electronic devices. This shift from time spent with the neighbourhood/ street or park peer group or just hanging out at the mall has left many youth entering university or the workforce with little, if any, informal experience with their age mates — especially those experiences not directed by an adult. Such changes are playing out at home, school, work, play and community living. In this book we have tried to help you identify the strengths and weaknesses of these new realities so that you can more effectively manage the tasks of your groups in all these situations.

In closing, I'd like to thank Irene Devine for her contribution to the previous edition of this book, most of which is included here. Raye Kass has written Part VI with its three focused reports on new group theory and practice with her graduate students and her consulting with multicultural groups, especially the high risk groups in space programs. Thanks also to the team at Captus Press for making this edition's publication and use fully effective.

Hedley G. Dimock
September 2011

The New Realities of Workgroups in the Digital Age and Globalization

R aye and I mentioned in our preface that almost half of the content of this edition was written for or refocused in response to the new realities of workgroups in the "digital age" and globalization. Let us start then by identifying and understanding these new group factors and the challenges they bring to making workgroups more effective.

THE NEW GROUP FACTORS FOR THE DIGITAL AGE

Demographically, the baby boomers are starting to retire but as the recent recession reduced their retirement funds, many have come back to contract or part-time jobs. Seniors' numbers have continued to increase along with their influence in society. But the enormous change has been the ubiquity — everywhere at the same time — of the digital generation (1977–1998). Most people you see in the mall or in the classroom, or walking somewhere are on their cell phones or electronic devices. The impact of the constant use of these has changed the structure of many workgroups.

The skills of this digital generation in using their computers and related electronic devices — to collect and handle information; and to analyze, scrutinize, and quickly problem solve with the information (practised in video games) — are changing everything. This generation are the leaders and experts in these worldwide changes. It has changed how they learn, work, and communicate.

Since many of our readers are equipped with these skills and behaviours, let us remind you of your impact on education where you can access information faster and better than your teachers and have more powerful tools than most universities and other organizations with your Google, blogs, news sites, Facebook, Myspace, and Twitter. As you learn electronically, you are making hard copy textbooks irrelevant. And as most universities do not quickly address these realities or your new ways of learning, they still use the telling principles of child-focused pedagogy, ignoring a revolution in the making.

E-mail has replaced voice phone calls as well as faxes and continues to take over more communication here and worldwide. Digital communication influenced every candidate's run for president in the 2008 U.S. election and the "net kids" were credited with electing Barack Obama president. Outside direction of demonstrations and terrorist attacks are now run by electronic devices since cell phones can be blocked and traced. It is unlikely that any previous generation has been as empowered so early in their life. With these new realities, of course, come a number of new challenges for our effective group works and we'll get to those shortly.

Women in the workforce have continued to make gains in their striving for equality with men. The majority of students in university and the majority of entrepreneurs of small businesses are women. They are taking over some professions such as medicine where they are outnumbering men in medical schools. They are moving toward equality in higher education and even making strides in heavy industry. During the 2008–2010 recession, a lower percentage of women lost their jobs than men. These advances, and especially into previously male-dominated occupations, have made the role of women a new reality in the workgroups generally and especially those of global multicultural composition. The radically differing views of the "appropriate roles, behaviour, and dress of women" in different cultures will be discussed, and effective management suggestions described as another of the new challenges.

We have talked a bit about the new realities of digital communication and learning styles and their impact on workgroups. There are two additional realities that are closely related and confound the focus of this challenge. The first is the rapid increase in the number of illiterate Canadians. More than 40 percent of Canadians and over 50 percent in many areas don't have the ability to read this paragraph or the microwave instructions for frozen foods. Writing a report is also unmanageable for them.

However, most of these illiterate people are competent in their native language and have some to considerable verbal skills in English or French, and this muddles the challenge further. Group members with the same first language may subgroup and seek/demand the right to work in that language. Small groups with a similar language and culture can be a major influence on the sociometry of the group. "Birds of a feather flock together", and this is the second issue to muddle the reality with illiteracy.

Two outstanding features of globalization form the new realities that affect our workgroups. First, they are creating educational programs that are global in scope and will equip students to live usefully in our multicultural Canadian society and to work anywhere in the world. The second half of this global/multicultural reality is changing our Canadian institutions — social and cultural — and more specifically our workgroup leadership and management skills. This is an especially important dynamic in Canada because of our strong commitment and universal sensibility to the growing pluralistic, multisocial, and multicultural character of our society.

While globalization/multiculturalism, demographics, and digital revolution are the major focus of the new realities in this book, there are a few other we'd like to mention.

The increasing competition among the growing number of human service organizations plus the recent economic recession and its slow recovery has put additional pressures on these organizations. These pressures have resulted in some organizations neglecting their reason for existing just to survive. Mergers and acquisitions are one result. Another result is a shifting focus such as universities pushing research, which is paid by the project, at the expense of students who are paid for equally regardless of the quality of teaching and extracurricular services. And new issues have surfaced: environmental concerns, social and ethical behaviour of and in organizations, and the lack of responsibility in government, organizations, and society in general — the "no one is accountable for anything" syndrome. These factors have combined in such a way that human service organizations have little or no interest in evaluating the effectiveness of their programs and efforts to achieve their mission and goals with credible results and outcomes. Consequently, their programs have no impetus to respond to these new realities. Maybe, in desperation to appear current, they will "put the old wine in new bottles", and hope they can wiggle their way through this period of "resting on their oars".

Yesterday I was passing a stranger of about 60 years old who was climbing a small hill to get to the sidewalk where I was. As he tramped through the snow I said, "Ah, blazing a new trail are you?" He quickly replied that he was testing his new knee he finally got from the veterans administration, thanks to the new political party in power. In short, he reported how the previous party cared nothing for the military force (he had come up from private to major) and wouldn't fix his injury or give him a pension. But, he said, "We fixed them. When they (the previous government) told us soldiers what to do, we said 'yes sir, right away' and continued doing everything just as we had always done it."

I believed him to be typical of many of the over-30 age group who are going to resist these new realities and hold back the effective use of the concepts and procedures described in this book.

In this new edition we have had to change the concept and our understanding of the word "group". While the original definition is still valid — two or more people in a state of communication — the physical and technological dimensions have changed. We no longer have the expectation that the group will work face-to-face and communicate verbally by word of mouth. These groups used coffee breaks, lunches, and after-work or out-of-school parties and activities for group building and "off the record" worthwhile planning. The personal status of group members overrode that of the system and the influence of the group, as a cohesive unit, ran circles around the formal organization.

Now, and increasingly in the future, we have some groups that do not meet face-to-face, and some that meet occasionally but do most of their work and social networking as individuals. Cell phones are used for some of the communication, but use of the digital tools such as Facebook and Twitter is increasing. While there is still a lot of social networking (and some digital dating), the kind of leadership and coaching useful in "making workgroups effective" is changing.

WHERE DO THESE NEW REALITIES LEAVE US?

To make a long story short, we have tried to present these new realities as straightforwardly as possible. Readers from the digital generation who have grown up with these dynamics may be saying "so what else is new?" Nevertheless, the adults in our life — parents, grandparents, teachers, coaches, etc. — have not done so and the leading and managing styles and techniques they modelled for you may not work for you. The culture (usual ways of doing things) of their era has required updating, much of it by law and edict. Working with them — your parents, professors, friends, and superiors — will be your workgroup challenge.

For the baby boomers and us seniors, the challenge is to know and understand the pros and cons, and accept the new realities. This doesn't mean liking them necessarily, as the jury is still out about their long-term value. Canada is strongly committed to being a pluralistic and multicultural society and bending over with sensitivity to its issues. The demographic shifts and digital revolution have already happened and can only continue though their pace may slow down or speed up.

There is much excitement, yet some ambivalence and anxiety as the older-than-30 workforce move to manage these challenges. Flexibility in our usual ways of doing things; tolerance of differences in attitudes, dress, and values; and motivation to be creative and experimental in trying out new ways of working are the tried and true places to start. This also likely means reducing our expectations about the time, comfort, and energy it will take to accomplish our collaborative workgroup tasks.

On a personal level, Hedley has found it very helpful as a senior citizen and lifelong student of groups to describe and consider the impact of these challenges. Hopefully, this learning will be apparent in making the new edition of this book more useful to you all, its readers.

Understanding Group Behaviour

2

GROUP LEADERSHIP

The most important and exciting interest in a group is its leadership — who is providing it and how well it is working out. The way in which the leader works with the group and the impact of that style on the group's productivity and the satisfaction and relationships of members have been a focus of continuous study for many years. Style of leadership has been found to be closely related to learning in classrooms, production in industry, achievement in team sports, growth in therapy groups, and task accomplishment in the military. Clearly, an understanding of group leadership is a priority for everyone working with groups. Everyone has ideas about leadership — how people get to be leaders and what leaders should do to be successful and effective. Let's look at the understandings about leadership that will help us to put these divergent assumptions and attitudes into a bit of perspective.

The earliest major theory of leadership was that in every group there was one leader and that this person was the leader because of certain leadership traits or leadership qualities. This was called the "great man" theory of leadership as it was believed that there were certain men (women were generally not included in this theory at that time) who were destined to become great leaders because they possessed outstanding traits and abilities. Leadership was thought to be a talent like singing or dancing that some people were born with but others did not have. Alexander the Great, Hannibal, Julius Caesar, Benjamin Franklin, Napoleon, and Winston Churchill were frequently mentioned in this regard. The major events in history were also thought to have revolved around these great leaders and history could be best understood by studying them. It was also thought that these people were born with these outstanding qualities or traits and that they would be leaders regardless of the time or place in which they lived.

The question then was "What are these special traits that leaders have?" Early studies of leadership tried to identify these traits but every time a set of characteristics was identified and looked promising, it was found not to work out in other settings. The search for leadership traits has been unsuccessful as years of research have been unable to find any consistent trait or personal characteristics which distinguish leaders from non-leaders. The conclusion has been that leaders do not have special personalities or traits, identifiable at this time, that separate them from other people. Certain personality variables are associated with effective leadership, but for the most part leadership is not a birthright or hereditary. The "trait approach" or "leaders are born" theory has been generally abandoned because of a lack of scientific support. Yet, many individuals continue to believe in it and continue, usually within the confines of their own workplace, to seek out the characteristics that identify their successful workers.

Leadership is now seen as a function of the situation — the type and difficulty of the task; the personality, motivation, and competence of the members; and the power of the leader. This *situational leadership* theory assumes that leaders may have certain traits or skills that will increase the probability of their becoming a leader but these characteristics may be important only in that situation. As leadership is related to the situation there is a fair probability that the leader in one situation will be a leader in another very similar situation but not if the situation is different.

Our experiences usually confirm this idea that the person who is the leader in one situation may not be the leader in another. A university class may see Jane as the leader in a classroom discussion as she is articulate and knows her subject matter, while Susan takes over in the planning of the class's end-of-year party using her social skills and entertainment interests. In the work team, the members may look to Estelle to help resolve a conflicted planning issue, and to Charles to make up the complicated shift schedule for the next month. And as we look at United States history we see some men who were outstanding military generals but were not very effective presidents.

During World War II, there was an increased interest in identifying potential leaders so that they could be given special training to increase their effectiveness. The German army continued to develop its "leaderless discussion" technique to select men for officers' training. Candidates were assembled in small groups and given a general topic to discuss. No one was appointed leader but observers rated each participant's behaviour on a number of criteria. A high rating on leadership in this leaderless group was found to have a positive correlation with army performance. Later, the British and American armies adopted this technique. The American army continued to use personality and performance tests but also experimented with numerous functional tests in selecting trainees for special missions overseas (OSS). These included stress situations such as frustrating instruction tasks, role playing and simulations of actual situations, and secret observation during drinking parties and other informal situations.

These studies stimulated an interest in exploring the functions of leaders, as leadership was seen as doing something to help a group solve a problem or accomplish an objective. Members perform leadership functions as they influence the behaviour of other members and help the group achieve its goals. Most members of a group are "leaders" then, at one time or another, and we must study the group as a whole and identify patterns of leadership or frequency of leadership acts. Assumptions that one person was the leader and the rest were followers were discontinued in this functional, shared leadership approach.

Functions of Group Leaders

The search for leadership functions continued in the late 1940s and 1950s at Ohio State University with Navy funding. These studies shaped our understanding of leadership and are still the basis for the most widely accepted leadership theories. In these studies four factors appeared consistently to describe leadership behaviour: showing consideration, initiating structure, emphasizing production, and showing social sensitivity. Showing consideration for other group members accounted for 50 percent of the leadership functions and initiating structure accounted for 30 percent.

The studies concluded that there are two basic leadership functions: (i) helping the group to accomplish a specific task; and (ii) helping to maintain or build the group itself. Goal achievement or task accomplishment functions include: defining roles and expectations for members; establishing defined structures for operating; initiating action; providing expert information; and evaluating goal achievement progress.[1] Group building and maintenance functions were showing concern for individuals, giving recognition and approval, facilitating open communication, providing support and encouragement, and stimulating self-direction.

It is clear that many members in a group may perform these functions, and some may even specialize in task functions, while others contribute group-building behaviours. Many behaviours can contribute to goal achievement and group building at the same time. Providing top notch plans for implementing a group task will not only increase goal achievement but also increase group solidarity and member satisfaction. Mediating a group conflict helps to maintain the group but also may free a log jam and move the group to accomplishing its task.

The generally agreed-upon characteristics of effective leaders at the end of the 20th century are shown in **Figure 1**.

In the 21st century, human service organizations have continued the quest to identify effective leaders. The preferred approach now

---

FIGURE 1 Functions of an Effective Leader

Goal Achievement	Group Maintenance
• technical skills	• social and interpersonal skills
• administrative skills	• social nearness, friendliness
• task motivation and application	• group task supportiveness
• leadership achievement	• maintaining cohesive workgroup
• maintaining standards of performance	• facilitating coordination and teamwork

• intellectual and communication skills

---

[1] An observation guide showing these functions is found in Dimock & Kass's *How to Observe Your Group*, one of nine books in this series.

appears to be split between the personal (face-to-face) interview and technological, psychological testing. Intelligence tests and personality tests, such as the Myers-Briggs, are most frequently used. The use of simulated group activity situations on video that required the candidate to make an intervention was gaining interest at the turn of the century but has fizzled out, at least in Canada. The jury is still out on what, if any, are the exact measurable characteristics of good leaders.

Managerial Roles and Behaviours

Our recent 2008 book, *Leading and Managing Dynamic Groups*, distinguished between leaders and managers and their usual roles and behaviours. Leaders are thinking beyond the present and have a vision for the future. They rethink present assumptions and practices and are always seeking new and better ways of doing things. Managers accept the situation as currently defined and work within the present structure and guidelines. They organize affairs to accomplish the work of the group efficiently and economically.

To help us get a grasp of the roles of managers, we have used a list of 10 roles that have been shown in **Figure 1** but made two additions, shown in italics, to manage the new realities **(Figure 2)**. We have enlarged the negotiator role to include, or perhaps focus on, arbitration and mediation. Our multicultural groups are loaded with divergent attitudes, beliefs, and behaviours, and the arising group conflicts and tensions require skilled management. This is an extremely important maintenance role to prevent the group from splitting into two or more non-functioning subgroups. It is usually handled by mediation — finding common ground that can be tolerated by all members — or arbitration — making an arbitrary decision and requiring members to

---

FIGURE 2 Three Categories of Managerial Roles

Interpersonal	Informational	Decisional
• Figurehead	• Monitor	• Entrepreneur
• Leader	• Disseminator	• Disturbance handler
• Liaison	• Spokesperson	• Negotiator/*Arbitrator*
• *Tolerator*		

act accordingly. The word *tolerate* has been used to suggest that the ideal of *accepting* consensus-based group decisions is great, but not functional in managing many divisive issues.

The relative importance of these roles varies with managerial level and function. Thus, a professor may perform some of the roles but not others, and a hospital administrator might perform still others. Each of these 12 roles is placed in one of the three general categories: interpersonal; informational; or decisional.

The first category of interpersonal roles is directly related to the authority of managers' positions and involves developing and maintaining positive relationships with a variety of significant people and groups. For example, the figurehead role entails responsibility for representing the organization in a variety of social, legal, and symbolic matters from presiding over the annual employee awards ceremonies to attending the wedding of a subordinate to taking an important customer to lunch. The leader role focuses on guiding organizational members toward accomplishing organizational goals. Some aspects have to do with staffing and others with motivating and/or coaching employees. The liaison role involves establishing links between the managers' organizations and factors outside their organization such as clients, government officials, members of boards of directors, and suppliers. The role of tolerator has been discussed as essential to managing the different attitudes, beliefs, behaviours, and styles of dress and appearance of members. Tolerance is also part of the informational role in using appropriate communication with the functionally illiterate and checking back for understanding perhaps several times. In our experience illiterate people usually hide this disability, saying they understand something when they don't. Tolerance for the time and skill that may be needed to handle the language differences and need for translation is the other part of its informational connection.

Tolerance also fits into the decisional role as we have also mentioned. It is especially important here as making group decisions is the most likely activity to bring to the surface the irreconcilable differing attitudes and beliefs among members; a cool head is required to negotiate and mediate anything acceptable. The frustration of trying to find common ground for an hour or two and still ending with an argumentative statement is discouraging, to say the least. As is spending a great deal of time negotiating and then having to accept a very low quality group decision.

These interpersonal roles make it possible for managers to build the networks that are crucial to carry out the next set of roles, the informational roles which refer to receiving and transmitting information and building networks of contacts for sharing information. Included in this category are the monitor role, the disseminator role, and the spokesperson role. Managers have to focus on assessing group and/or organizational performance by receiving and screening information and by scanning the environment for information that may affect the unit's performance. Decisions about the value of the information that is received and whether or not to use the information have to be made, as well as decisions about how much information is useful to share and distribute to subordinates and others in the organization. Managers also transmit information to relevant others outside the group or organization, such as the difference between an associate and full professor, or the group's action plans.

Perhaps the most important of the three categories of roles are decisional roles that involve making significant decisions that affect the organization. Four roles describe the manager as a decision-maker. These are the entrepreneur role, the disturbance handler role, the resource allocator role, and the negotiator/arbitrator role.

The entrepreneur role involves the design and initiation of planned change. A manager who seeks to improve an organizational position by initiating new products and services, or by implementing a survey to test a new service, product, or market, is engaging in the entrepreneur role. The negotiator and the resource allocator roles are closely linked and refer to the process of determining where resources will be placed to benefit the organization best. Settling disputes between organizational members and dealing with involuntary situations and changes such as strikes by labour, bankruptcy of major suppliers, or breaking of contracts by customers is also part of this category. The new realities, as mentioned, have brought more intergroup disputes and subgroup antagonisms, making group decisions more painful to manage. These different dynamics have made negotiation, mediation, and arbitration much more important roles for the management of small classroom groups and larger workgroups in human service organizations.

In some of these roles, a manager is making choices among competing demands for money, equipment, personnel, and access to management's time. What proportion of the budget should be earmarked for advertising and what proportion for improving existing programs? Should a second shift be added or should overtime be paid to handle new requests for products and services?

Although the categories of general roles and specific roles are quite arbitrary and do overlap, they provide some insight into the activities that leaders as managers perform and the skills that they are likely to need in order to carry out their work effectively.

Transformational Leadership and Management

Another way of looking at the functions of leaders and managers is through transactional and transformative distinctions. Transactional leaders motivate subordinates to perform at expected levels by helping them recognize their task responsibilities, identify goals, acquire confidence about meeting the expected performance levels, and understand how their needs and the rewards they expect are linked to goal achievement.

Let's consider John who sees himself as a good leader. He meets with subordinates to clarify expectations — what is required of them and what they can expect in return. As long as they meet his expectations, John doesn't bother them. Job performance is viewed as a series of transactions with subordinates — exchanging rewards for completed tasks or punishment for inadequate performance. The power that John uses comes from his organizational position and formal authority.

In contrast, transformational leaders motivate individuals to perform beyond normal expectations by creating a vision of what should be, by building commitment to that vision, and by facilitating changes that support the vision. Transformational leaders build confidence in their followers' abilities to achieve the extraordinary missions articulated by the leader.

Jodi is this different kind of leader. She has frequent face-to-face chats with each of her employees. When facing a crisis, she inspires her group's involvement and participation in the outcome. She solidifies it with simple words and images and keeps reminding her staff about it. She is a consultant, coach, and teacher. Her goal is to get subordinates to transform their own self-interest into the interest of the group through concern for a broader goal. The power that she uses is ascribed to personal characteristics like charisma, interpersonal skills, hard work, or personal contacts rather than to organizational status.

John, a transactional leader, may inspire a reasonable degree of involvement, loyalty, commitment, and performance from his subordinates. But Jodi, using a transformational approach, can do much more. Transformational leadership is not a substitute for transactional leadership but rather a supplemental form, namely, performance beyond expectations.

Transformational leadership is closely related to concepts like charismatic leadership or inspirational leadership. Lee Iacocca is often used as an example of a successful transformational leader because of his successful efforts in transforming Chrysler Corporation from a floundering company into one that was much more successful.

Women's Style of Leading

Some authors have noted that the transformational leadership style is based on relationship building, open communication, and team building, and that it tends to be more consensual than the more traditional command-and-control military model of leadership.

We are beginning to see more of this style of leadership now that more women are attaining senior management and leadership positions. Although not all women lead in this style and this is not to say that men cannot have this style, the transformational style does emphasize characteristics that are traditionally associated with women.

Whereas previous leadership studies focused on differences in the traits and leadership styles of women and men, and on stereotyped expectations imposed on women with respect to their leadership ability, more recent studies of women describe their unique style of leadership. At its core, these principles of women's style of leadership result in a style that differs from the traditional style in its reliance on emotional as well as rational data. Women are more likely to consider feelings as well as facts in making decisions and to strive for solutions in which everyone is a winner. Women are also more apt to be concerned with maintaining close personal relationships with others.

Naturally, these qualities aren't equally pronounced in all women managers and leaders, nor are they totally absent in all male leaders and managers. However, as a growing body of evidence suggests, women, as a group, compared to most men, do indeed have a different natural style of management and leadership, and are likely to function somewhat differently, yet effectively, in leadership roles.

Other Characteristics of Leaders

In youth groups, physical size has some relation to leadership potential and it is likely that this is related to athletic success where size may be an important factor. In adult situations, size does not appear to be significantly related to leadership, yet until the 1970s, police units in Canada had a minimum height and weight requirement, thinking that larger people got more respect and had more control in mass demonstrations (they gave up this requirement when it was shown to discriminate against several minority groups, including native Canadians — and women). As the studies of functions have shown, leaders tend to have more intelligence, insight, initiative, soundness of judgment, and originality. They likely have more energy (better physical health), a sense of humour, and may be a bit more tidy and attractive in their appearance than other members of the group.

It also appears that the person who does the most talking is most likely to influence the group and become accepted as leader, as long as that person doesn't talk so much as to antagonize other members. Those who emerge as leaders are usually more vocal and dominant and this may help the group to move toward its goals. Certainly, any member of a group who is the usual channel of communication, who has special access to people in power or influence related to the group's goals, or who controls communication in any way is more likely to be a leader than one who does not. This explains why discussion leaders, group recorders or reporters, or those whose job or interests puts them into frequent contact with other members have a tendency to become leaders. This seems more true for men than women. Although the gender gap in leadership has narrowed in recent years, it is still open to discrimination in many cultures. We will elaborate on this difference in the section on group structure.

An extensive study of high school basketball teams and several adult groups found that the leaders of the effective groups had greater social distance from their followers than the leaders of ineffective groups. Other studies also suggest that it may be better to be slightly aloof rather than "one of the gang". Later studies showed that the aloof leaders had a high goal achievement orientation and this helped them to have an effective group. It still seems social distance has some merits. While members still respect a leader with whom they are friendly and familiar, a leader who is too close to the members may find it difficult to realistically assess the strengths and weaknesses of individuals and tends to make decisions based on general personal feelings.

For example, the captains of the winning basketball teams were able to differentiate among their teammates on a variety of personal and skill dimensions. They could describe a comprehensive set of weaknesses and strengths for each player and did not tend to describe several players in a similar way. They knew who could dribble the best, who played well under pressure, who was a team player and got others passing the ball around, and who to put into the game if the team was behind and needed a "spark plug" to get it clicking.

In the human relations training programs of our centre, we worked at helping human service workers develop these skills of being able to differentiate among their employees, students, or clients. During their training programs we asked them to write a brief thumbnail sketch of the other members of their training group, or to write three adjectives descriptive of each of the other members. To check the usefulness of these descriptions we asked participants to read their descriptions and see if the other members could identify who they were talking about. Many participants used the same descriptions in reference to several members. Clearly, they found it difficult to see other participants as unique individuals and likely in their concern for their own well-being saw other members as "them". The participants who were able to describe others with such accuracy that other members could consistently recognize them usually were influential members or leaders in their groups. The need to be known and recognized as a unique person is an overwhelming motivation of adolescents but also is a major concern of youth and adults. Anyone who can recognize and identify the unique attributes of others gains considerable respect and often leadership status in their groups. On-the-job studies have indicated that this is true of leaders, youth workers, nurses, counsellors, and team leaders or managers. It seems to be especially true of emergent leaders in project or case study groups in university classrooms where there is no designated leader and is especially useful in multicultural groups.

The ability to inspire a shared vision is another characteristic of successful leaders that has been receiving considerable attention in recent years. Often we think of the visionary leader as someone starting a religious or political movement such as Billy Graham, Martin Luther King, or Mao. This ability to describe a mission or goal in such an attractive and exciting way that other people want to join in and go to work on it quickly identifies leaders. This ability can also mean the difference between winning and losing. In the 1970s, Pierre Trudeau's popularity was often attributed to his charisma (and more recently

Barack Obama) — his ability to clearly articulate his personal agenda in a way that inspired other people. Lee Iacocca could turn around the faltering Chrysler Corporation in the 1980s by inspiring a vision of success and empowering a critical mass of employees to work toward it. And in the 1990s, Bill Clinton was able to beat Bush by continually harping on his vision for a new future, while Bush appeared to stand for the status quo. The same was true in the 2008 U.S. election, as Obama did the same to Hillary Clinton and John McCain. (Some thought these were just cases of young candidates inspiring youth, yet more seniors voted for Clinton than Bush, and more for Obama than McCain.)

After motivating others with an inspiring mission or dream for the future, it is essential to initiate action toward these goals and involve others in the process. Dreams are a dime a dozen. It is the involvement of people in implementing them that makes the difference. Action toward new goals involves changing the way things usually happen — the customs, values, and traditions of behaviour of the group or organization. Change always involves risks and the person likely to earn leadership status will be a high risk-taker. The would-be leader will also be able to sustain the action initiated toward the goal by empowering others. This means being up front, being committed, and taking responsibility. Having power and influence from an assigned or designated position (director, supervisor, or manager) is most helpful in facilitating this sequence of inspiring others with a vision and then initiating and sustaining action toward it. However, we have frequently noted in our classroom that in project groups where there is no designated leader, the emergent leader is the person who has been able to describe best how the group can accomplish its task, have some fun, and get a good grade.

Leadership and the Group

If leadership is best thought of as a group quality or set of functions which are needed for the group to operate effectively, then the interrelations among members must be studied to understand why certain members more frequently perform these functions. Or, to put it differently, leadership and the relation of the leader to followers cannot be looked at independently. The leader derives that position from the followers who see the leader as being able to help them to achieve this goal and maintain themselves as a group. The more a person helps other members accomplish their objectives, the more readily will these members accept that person's suggestions and look to that leader for further suggestions and help in building the solidarity of the group. Leaders may emerge as they appear to be able to provide for group needs or they may be selected because they control the means or resources (skills, knowledge, money, equipment, contacts, etc.) which the group needs to gain its objectives. Even if the leader is appointed by someone outside the group, the leader's status and acceptability will depend on the group's perspective of the person's ability to meet group needs or at least prevent reduced need satisfaction.

Accumulated studies have now made it clear that leadership is a function of group needs and that leaders emerge or should be assigned to groups on the basis of group needs and not on the basis of the leader's previous experiences, length of service, or general accomplishments. Leaders, in fact, are most effective if they integrate and personify the norms of the group. This really makes the leader the "follower" of the group.

It appears that to gain status and acceptance in a group an individual must conform to the standards of the group upon entering the group. Once this person has demonstrated an acceptance of the group's norms and can make contributions to the group's achievement of goals within these norms, status increases rapidly. Once a high status position is achieved, it is possible to deviate from traditional practices and establish new norms or ways of working.

A most interesting study conducted some years ago illustrates this point rather well. Children from 4 to 11 years of age were formed into a dozen homogeneous age groups. Each group met for several sessions until it had institutionalized certain procedures such as seating positions, permanent division of toys, ceremonies connected with group play, sequences of games, and so forth. Then a leader of about the same age was put into the group. These leaders had been selected on the basis of their status in previous groups. Generally, the new leader tried to do away with group traditions and show it new ones. The leader was rejected by the group but quickly made an about-face, accepted the group's traditions, and learned considerable skills in those traditions. At this point the new leader was able to introduce modifications into established traditions and gradually introduce new ways of working into the group. Although the new leaders had previously demonstrated more competence than any of their group members, they had to accept and personify the traditions of the group before they gained enough power to start to modify them. Clearly, leaders depend on the group for their power.

There is little possibility of a person influencing a group without being influenced by it, or of directing it toward an end not accepted by the members. The leader is interdependent with the other members and before the members will be influenced by the leader, he or she must have demonstrated an acceptance of group norms and traditions. The chief exception is when the leader derives considerable power from outside the group and may be able to coerce members toward unacceptable objectives. This assumption that leadership is a function of the group and that the group's norms control everyone including the leader helps to explain why many groups change very little when a new leader takes over.

In fact, many writers on leadership have suggested that the job should be built around the leader rather than assigning the leader to do the job. This makes sense if you believe that leadership is a function of the situation and very much controlled by the culture and traditions of the organization. This group of writers also believes that managerial effectiveness is more likely to be improved by working at changing the culture — the usual ways of doing things — than by training the manager in more effective ways of working or by replacing the manager. The usual criteria for hiring or promoting to another job, such as educational credentials, personality, and previous track record, are only somewhat relevant if the leader is seen as a product of the followers and the situation.

When Hedley started a new university department, instead of hiring staff to teach specific courses as universities usually do, he hired the people and encouraged them to develop the courses they would like to teach and that were very relevant to the mission of the department. All of these new professors developed new courses and programs, several of which had never been taught in a Canadian university. The discussion of whether we fit the leader to the job or the job to the leader will, we think, continue for some time.

Leadership Style

The collapse of the "great man" and trait theories of leadership gave rise to the assumption that leaders were made and not born. As this idea was developed further there became a surge of activity to investigate how people developed certain leadership styles and what impact these styles had on other people — group members, workers, clients, students, and family members. The focus of the first studies was on the authoritarian personality and comparisons of authoritarian and democratic leadership. Following the Ohio State studies and the emergence of goal achievement and group maintenance as the two major dimensions of leadership, they became the focus for examining leadership style. The focus on leadership style comparing or combining goal achievement and group-building orientations represents the state-of-the-art today. Let's examine these orientations and assess the usefulness of their implications for increasing our ability to make groups more effective.

Dominating-Participative Styles of Leadership

One of the now classical studies in group leadership describes the effects of authoritarian and participative leadership on the behaviour of club members.[2] Small groups of 10-year-old boys were formed to work on theatrical mask making and other projects after school hours. In the first experiment there were two clubs and Lippitt led both, one in a dominating fashion and the other in a participative way. In the follow-up experiment four groups were formed and each one had a dominating and a participative leader for six-week periods. An attempt was made to equate the groups on a number of variables at the time of formation and the groups experienced the style of leadership in a different order to minimize further variables. Also, the team of adults took turns playing dominating and participative leaders to ensure that differences in the boys' recreations were due to the method of leadership and not the personality of the leader.

This experiment showed that the boys reacted toward each other in the same way the leader acted toward them. In groups that had an autocratic leader the members were more dominating and aggressive toward each other than in the participative groups. When the leader left the room the participative groups went right on working while the dominated clubs stopped work and fought to see who would replace the leader as authority figure. The children's behaviour and attitudes, as well as the extent to which they liked the club, were very closely related to the type of leadership.

In the participative clubs the members were more cooperative and behaviour was more constructive. There was more interaction,

---

[2] Ralph White and Ronald Lippitt, *Autocracy and Democracy*. New York: Harper, 1960.

friendliness, individuality, and creativeness, as well as high group cohesiveness. Hostility was 30 times as frequent in autocratic groups and members were more demanding and discontented. There was also more scapegoating of members and more dropped out of the clubs. Nine-tenths of the boys liked the dominating leader less than the participative leader. On the positive side, the autocratic groups produced a bit more in terms of completed projects and had less out-of-field conversation (the price participative groups paid for individuality and freedom).

During the following three decades numerous studies continued to contrast dominating with participative leadership style, assuming that leaders, managers, or teachers were either one or the other. Reviewing the results of these studies helps us to understand why there remains today such a stigma about directive leadership and why the acceptable leader uses a participative style.

Studies in classrooms showed that dominating teachers had a high proportion of unproductive behaviour in their classrooms and had students who were more self-centred, frustrated, hostile, and socially negative. In participative classrooms where the teachers were more relaxed and permissive, there was more friendly, cooperative, socially constructive, and healthy behaviour from students. While dominating teachers often had students who learned as much or more, the participative classrooms found greater changes in attitudes and behaviour, more growth in self-direction and confidence, and all-round healthier students.

The same general findings were substantiated in business and industry where supervisors who operated in a participative style, sharing responsibility and decision-making with their subordinates, had high production and good morale (low absenteeism and turnover). While recent studies indicate that production is not always higher under participative supervisors, there is still a strong value judgment that participative leadership is most desirable. This feeling has been encouraged by the quality of working life projects where the self-esteem of the worker receives considerable attention and by the Japanese quality work circles and Theory Z management styles.

The leadership style of parents has also been found to be a definite influence on children's behaviour and development. Participative-oriented parents have children who tend to be more stable emotionally, more creative, and better adjusted socially than children of authoritarian parents. Dominating parents have been linked to rigid conformity in their children and hostile feelings toward people in general. The 21st century has, however, showcased some of the problems of the Dr. Spock era baby boomers of participative, laissez faire parents, who are now often called the "entitled generation." More important than whether the leadership is directive or participative, we have now found that it is the consistency with which it is applied that counts. Both children and adults like to know what the rules of the game are and how they will be applied to their behaviour. Recent polls have found that many former East Germans long for the good old days of the autocratic Russian rule where they knew what was what and the rules didn't change from week to week.

Participative Leadership

The same group of people will behave in different ways when the leadership style of the designated leader changes. And the effectiveness of the group is closely related to the appropriateness of the leader's style to the group's situation. While the participative style has been found to work well in many situations, it is not always the most satisfactory. Directive leadership is effective in reaching high production goals in certain situations, is required in emergency situations, and found to be very expediting when people are working well and have a high level of trust. It is also expected when the task is straightforward and the leader is given responsibility for directing action such as the pilot in an airliner or the surgeon in an operating room. Participative leadership by sharing decision making and other responsibilities enables a group to make full use of all its members' potentials and increases self-esteem in the process. This is particularly important in restrictive work situations where jobs are dull and repetitive.

The early studies of participative leadership showed that it was a powerful factor in promoting personality development and personal growth in group situations. At that time Hedley was very involved in training workers in the human service professions and set out to develop a tool or procedure that would identify participative-oriented leaders. With such a tool it would be possible to see if participative leaders would do better in their work with groups than more dominating leaders. If the tool identified leaders as participative and they were found to be more successful, then the same tool could also be used to assess the success of training programs to produce effective leaders.

A wide variety of approaches to identifying participative-oriented leaders was tried out but the most successful was a pencil and paper attitude survey. It included some questions from the studies identifying the authoritarian personality, a cooperation scale from the Guilford-Zimmerman Temperament Survey, and some questions about leadership beliefs. The Dimock Leadership Inventory emerged and was found to measure a flexible, cooperative, participative orientation to working with others. It was validated on 350 people working in 15 small group leadership situations such as youth groups and summer camps. All the leaders completed the inventory in advance of their jobs and scores were correlated with on-the-job ratings given to them by their supervisor as part of a performance appraisal. While the results decisively illustrated that participative-oriented leaders were more successful as rated by their supervisors, it was not a continuous correlation. That is, the most participative leaders were not any better than the moderately participative leaders, but rather the authoritarian-oriented leaders were not successful and this was true more than nine times out of ten.

A few years after developing the Leadership Inventory, Hedley used it to check the studies that showed students in participative-led classrooms changed their attitudes and beliefs most (see **Table 1**). Thirty-one university classes, leadership training programs, and supervisory situations were studied with over 900 participants. The programs were divided into four categories based on the degree to which learners participated in the situation. All groups were rated on the amount of change the participants showed on the Dimock Leadership Inventory: no change, some change, or considerable change. The results shown in Table 1 confirm the previous research — participating in a learning experience facilitated a change in attitudes toward those found to be associated with on-the-job success. Again these studies showed that there was more attitude change from the low participation groups compared to the medium participation groups than from the medium participation to the very high participation groups. It seems learning does not increase steadily as participation increases, but that a shift from non-participation to at least moderate participation generates a significant increase. These findings of an optimum in participative leadership could be important as they would explain why the high participation orientations of humanistic education, child-centred parenting, self-actualizing therapy, and personal growth groups have not improved on the results of more moderate participation.

TABLE 1 Participation and Attitude Change Measured on the Dimock Leadership Inventory

		Amount of Member Participation in Class or Group			
		Low (N = 4)	Medium (N = 6)	High (N = 12)	Very High (N = 9)
Amount of Change	None	4	2	1	1
	Some	0	3	6	4
	A Lot	0	1	5	4

Goal Achievement and Group-Building Leadership Styles

The identification of two major dimensions of leadership in the Ohio State studies led to the development of two-dimensional leadership theories (the dominating-participative theory was one dimension) incorporating goal achievement orientation and group building/maintenance. These functional leadership theories saw leaders and, in fact, all group members assessed on their orientation or concern for goal achievement (also called task accomplishment or concern for production) and group building/maintenance (also called "concern for people" or relationships).

Thus we first look at how much concern or motivation a person has toward task accomplishment, and how much toward group building/maintenance. Suppose a person is rated as shown below:

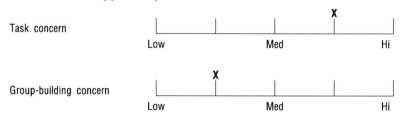

These ratings would now be combined on a two-dimensional matrix and general descriptions applied (**Figure 3**).

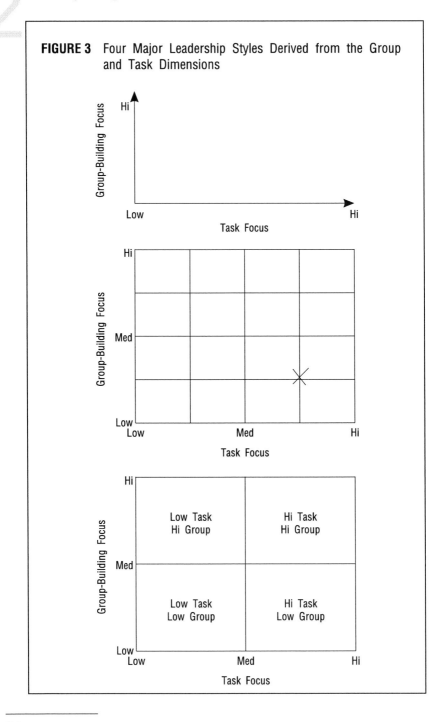

FIGURE 3 Four Major Leadership Styles Derived from the Group and Task Dimensions

The person described above would now be described as a high task, low group-building leader. Generally, this leadership theory as personified by the Blake Grid[3] assumed that there was a best leadership style and it was a high task, high group-building style, which had been supported by the Ohio State and related research. The one best style of leadership did not integrate well with the studies showing that leadership was a function of situational variables and new situational theories.

SITUATION LEADERSHIP THEORIES

Leadership is seen as a function of the situation and as the factors in the situation change, it is anticipated that different styles of leadership will be most effective. Thus one of the vital variables in the success of a group is the appropriateness of the leader's style to the situation. In considering this match between the leadership style and the situation, these theories propose that it is the situation that should determine the style. Or, as we said earlier, it is the followers that set the scene and expectations for the leader.

The most useful of the situational theories add a third dimension to our previous two of goal achievement and group building, and it assesses the appropriateness of the style on these two dimensions for the situation, specifically the maturity of the groups.

The important implication of the addition of this situational appropriateness dimension is that no one best leadership style remains, as the effectiveness of the style varies with the situation. Groups benefit from leadership that meshes with the needs of their members. Thus in some situations a high task style will be best while at other times a high group-building style will be most appropriate. The development of these theories by Hersey, Blanchard, and Johnson (2007) clarifies that leaders can increase their effectiveness by enlarging their repertoire of leadership styles and not be confined to the same style as the needs and situations change. And by developing their skills in diagnosing the situations they are working in, leaders can make better choices of the appropriate style to use. As a leader becomes more flexible and comfortable in using a variety of leadership styles, and becomes more competent in diagnosing leadership situations and plugging in the most

---

[3] R. Blake and J. Mouton, "How to Choose a Leadership Style", *Training and Development Journal*, 36(2) (February 1982), 39–47.

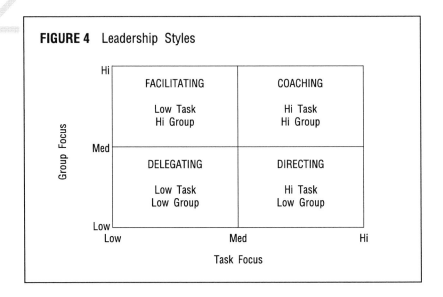

FIGURE 4 Leadership Styles

Group Focus (vertical axis): Hi, Med, Low
Task Focus (horizontal axis): Low, Med, Hi

FACILITATING Low Task Hi Group	COACHING Hi Task Hi Group
DELEGATING Low Task Low Group	DIRECTING Hi Task Low Group

appropriate style, that leader's effectiveness will increase. Let's see how it works.

We have the two dimensions of goal achievement (which we'll call TASK for task accomplishment), and group building/maintenance (which we'll shorten to GROUP). These are combined into a two-dimensional form as shown in **Figure 3**. In **Figure 4**, the form is divided into four squares for an overview. They represent four major combinations of the two dimensions and propose four major leadership styles. Using these four leadership style names will make it easier to talk about them (see **Figure 4**.)

Style

Most leaders have a style that they prefer to use, and in the hundreds of human service staff groups with whom we've worked it is a coaching style (high task, high group). Some staff typically use a directing style and others use a facilitating style but very few in our studies prefer the delegating style. All four styles can be equally useful as each of the four is most effective in certain situations. The well-rounded leader would ideally be equally comfortable and skilful in each of the four basic styles.

Directing
This style involves initiating and providing structure (how and when things will be done), providing clear directions about what is to be done and expectations about quantity and quality (defining roles and expectations), providing information about the environment or organization within which the group operates, evaluating and monitoring task accomplishment, and generally emphasizing goal achievement.

Coaching
This style involves continuing to provide much of the structure, task emphasis, and monitoring/evaluating functions of the directing style, but does so as a coach rather than a boss. Additional roles are providing support and encouragement, showing personal interest in member's well-being, seeking more reaction and feedback from the members, and generally establishing supportive, personal relationship with followers.

Facilitating
This style involves followers in making the decisions that affect them and facilitating their problem solving and decision-making activities, providing social/emotional support, coordinating group activities, mediating and harmonizing interpersonal problems, building strong, cohesive relationships within groups, and generally building harmonious, personally enhancing relationships with followers.

Delegating
This style involves delegating responsibility and accountability to followers and then letting them do their jobs, giving recognition for noteworthy accomplishments, protecting members from outside trivia, and liaising with related groups or parts of the organization on followers' behalf, and generally demonstrating trust and confidence in followers' ability to accomplish the task and maintain themselves as a healthy, viable group.

The Effectiveness Dimension
Although it's recognized that most people have a preferred style of leadership, flexibility, if it is consistent, rather than constant use of one style is the hallmark of effective leadership.

Establishing which of these four styles is likely to be the most appropriate depends on an accurate diagnosis of the situation at a given time. We say "at a given time" because a group that has worked together for some time may experience different needs and pressures as new members join the group, as the group moves to a new location, as its budget is cut or expanded, or as other groups move in to compete with the programs it provides.

In assessing situational factors there are no hard-and-fast rules but several factors continually emerge. Generally, the focus is on the *followers* and the *situation*. They are assessed on a poor–fair–good continuum.

> *Followers*: Competence of the members to accomplish the tasks or performance/knowledge skills, motivation to accomplish the tasks, previous experience or training with the task, and self-confidence in accomplishing the task. (Rate these items as poor, fair, or good.)

> *Situation*: Clarity of the task and how to accomplish it; general understanding of the environment, the usual ways of working, and expectations for group members; the personal power (how much the followers prefer and like the leader) and position power (ability to reward and punish the members) of the leader; and the quality of interpersonal relations within the group. (Rate these factors as poor, fair, or good.) **Figure 5** shows the style most likely to be effective given the rating of the situational factors.

Summary

Leaders will benefit from diagnosing the situational factors at a given time in the groups where they are providing leadership. As these factors move assessments from poor to fair, leaders will increase their group-building functions and shift their styles from one of directing to coaching and then to facilitating. As the situational factors move to good, it may be appropriate to move to a delegating style or, if the group is asking for direction and action, a directing style. Groups that "have it all together" may prefer to "run their own show" without a lot of over-the-shoulder help from the leader. Or they may prefer some direct action-taking and assignment of specific tasks as they trust the leader and want to eliminate lengthy planning meetings as they get on with the task to which they are all committed and competent to accomplish.

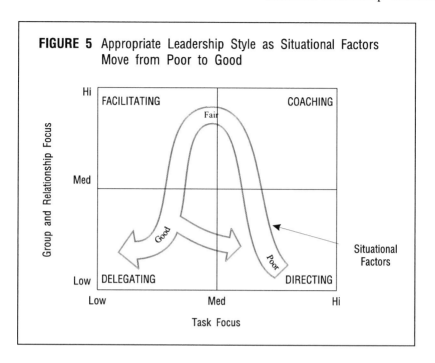

FIGURE 5 Appropriate Leadership Style as Situational Factors Move from Poor to Good

Some Implications

1. Starting a new group with the successful accomplishment of a task can be helpful. For many years Hedley's style was to start a new group in a facilitating style, helping people get to know one another and work out the ways they wanted to proceed with meeting their task accomplishment expectations. **Figure 5** (the model) suggests that this is appropriate for groups where the situational factors are fair but not where the factors are poor. As it is always best to start on the right side of the model (it is easier to give social/emotional rewards and status to participants than to take them away), he now starts with high structure and direction while assessing the situational factors and then moves to coaching and facilitating as quickly as these factors indicate.

2. Moving from one style to another should be done slowly and without skipping a style. It was Hedley's practice to provide an extensive orientation for new staff or students who reported to him (directing), but after they knew the job or course and its

31

expectations, he moved to a delegating style. This model helped him to understand why he needed to move into a coaching style, and then a facilitating style before leaving them to "sink or swim". As a colleague of ours often says "moving quickly from a directing style to a delegating style keeps the jails full".

3. These understandings help to focus on the alternative actions leaders should consider when their efforts to be helpful are not working well. This may highlight that a leader has difficulty providing the structure and direction that a new group of relatively unskilled people need (which may be why many people prefer working with older youth rather than with young children).

4. As the model is a developmental one, expecting that groups and individuals will grow and develop from poor situational factors to good situational factors, it focuses on the style the leader should be moving toward as the leader encourages this growth. Many leaders find it difficult to move from a coaching style to a facilitating style as it means giving up control. This is illustrated in many families where the greatest tension comes when adolescents are ready for a facilitating (low task, high relationship) style, but parents tend to remain in a coaching style that continues to monitor and evaluate activities and performance.

5. This also helps to explain why some leaders "rise to their level of incompetence" in an organization. A swimming pool instructor may establish a fine record of successes and be promoted to aquatics director for the agency. In her role of instructor she used her usual leadership style of a lot of direction with some support which was exactly what the situation called for. But as team leader of the aquatics staff, where the situational factors (staff competence and motivation, group solidarity) were fair to good, the high-task micromanaging approach was no longer successful. The staff resented the constant monitoring of their work and constant pressure; morale sank and there were frequent complaints from staff circulating through the agency. With a poor record as aquatics director, it is unlikely that she would be considered for a promotion and hence stays on in the aquatics position having "risen to her level of incompetence".

6. Irene's preferred style of university teaching usually depends on the followers, i.e., the group of students and their level in the program of studies. For example, with first year undergraduate students, she generally starts with a directing style since the students

lack the skill, competence, and knowledge in knowing the system, the program expectations, the norms, and the culture. As the course progresses and students gain confidence in task accomplishment and knowledge, she slowly moves to a coaching style. In teaching upper years of undergraduate students or MBA students, however, she generally starts with a coaching style and then moves to more of a facilitating style since these students tend to have more program experience and know what they want to learn. They are usually more motivated and more self-confident in task accomplishment than entering students. Assessing the situational factors assists Irene in determining the appropriate teaching style.

7. Following up from the previous example, it is evident that the followers and situation determine the appropriate leadership style. This should encourage us as leaders to diagnose these situational factors in a new job and, if they don't fit our usual leadership style, to consider whether we are prepared to change our style or should turn down the appointment to that situation. As supervisors we could consider the situational factors as part of selecting the most appropriate person for an assignment or new position. The supervisor of the aquatics instructor could be faulted for not being more aware of the likely inappropriateness of her usual style and of not providing the directing and coaching to help her make the transition.

8. We have highlighted the usefulness of all four leadership styles and the flexibility in their use in the development of a group. However, the changes in style need to stay consistent in their application and not leave members wondering what's going to happen today.

9. The new realities of the multicultural and digital revolution that we described in Part One are changing the rules of the game in applying these leadership principles. The difficulties that virtual digital groups have in building the level of trust and cohesion compared to face-to-face groups is an important change. Another is the clash of expected and preferred leadership styles and member roles and behaviour of different cultures now more frequently represented in groups.

    Raye's case example in Part Six about her "Semi-Virtual Teams in a Graduate Program" describes many of the new variables. Raye describes her dilemmas in attempting to manage these new situations. She attempts to help readers understand the different dynamics and suggest the directions in which she is headed. But as little credible research has been done in this area there are no clear remedial actions available.

SEX DIFFERENCES IN LEADERSHIP AND EFFECTIVENESS

During the past few decades the number of women hired, appointed, promoted, and elected to leadership positions has been increasing.

Leadership studies conducted in laboratory settings show that men seem to be more task-oriented whereas women are more interpersonal-oriented. As discussed previously, women tend to emphasize group solidarity, reduction of group tension, and avoidance of antagonism. Women, relative to men, perform more relationship-oriented actions and describe themselves as more relationship-oriented on questionnaires.

Studies conducted in actual organizational and group settings, however, generally find no gender differences in effective leadership performance. As managers, women tended to be both task- and relationship-oriented whereas men were primarily task-oriented. The only difference between men and women that emerges consistently across studies concerns participation: women generally use a participative leadership style whereas men tend to use more of a directive leadership style.

In the early seventies the studies conducted on gender differences in leadership indicated that many people expressed a preference for male bosses and many people assumed that men made better leaders than women, and they even gave men higher evaluations when men and women performed the same behaviours. It is important to note, however, that the majority of these studies on gender and leadership have depended on traditional theoretical models such as the trait, contingency, and situational approaches — and they have often used laboratory experiments with traditional instrumentation. Recent studies are more encouraging as they show less male favouritism and more satisfaction when their leader adopts a participative style or a relationship-oriented style and that gender per se has little impact on evaluations.

As gender roles continue to change in society, new questions will emerge, but we must conclude that the available literature suggests that the variables specified by the concepts and theories examined in this chapter, not gender, determine leadership effectiveness.

Sex Differences in Group Performance

There are two key factors that determine which sex excels in group performance: task content and interaction style. Groups of men are better at tasks that require mathematical expertise or physical strength or where the content of the task is more consistent with the typical skills, interests, and abilities of men rather than women. Groups of women excel at verbal tasks. Sex differences in group performance are also influenced by the differing interaction styles that men and women often adopt in groups. Because men more often enact a task-oriented interaction style, whereas women enact an interpersonally oriented interaction style, men outperform women when success is dependent on a high rate of task activity and women outperform men when success depends on a high level of interactive and collaborative activity. The research summarized from these studies were based on North American groups. Current research on groups that are more multisocial and multicultural may produce different results.

Attitudes versus Behaviour

Managers, school teachers, and graduate students in the social sciences have been found, in our experience, to be very interested in endless discussion of leadership styles and which ones they think are the most appropriate. Often such discussions start with comparisons of various assumptions they hold about the people with whom they worked. Many years ago Douglas McGregor summed up these attitudes as Theory X and Theory Y. Theory X leaders assume that people will only do as much as is required of them, and then only if they are closely monitored. Theory Y leaders believe that people can be self-directed and creative at work if properly motivated. Can't you just hear the graduate students arguing about how much work in a course their classmates would do if there was no term paper or final exam, and perhaps just a pass or fail rather than a letter grade? Think about how your assumptions about people measure up by using **Figure 6**.

In these debates Theory Y assumptions would usually prevail but not always. Managers of McDonald's and Burger King fast food outlets do not believe their entry-level employees would do much work without their presence and control, and university students usually favour a letter grade over a pass/fail non-grade in a specific course. In any case,

FIGURE 6 Assumptions about People

Assign a weight of 0–10 to each half of the following pairs of statements.

1. One problem in asking employees for their ideas is that their perspective is too limited for their suggestions to be of much practical value. _____ (X)

   Asking employees for their ideas broadens their perspective and results in useful suggestions. _____ (Y)

   Total 10

2. If you pay people enough money they are less likely to be concerned with such intangibles as responsibility and recognition. _____ (X)

   If you give people interesting and challenging work, they are less likely to complain about such things as pay and supplemental benefits. _____ (Y)

   Total 10

3. If people are allowed to set their own goals and standards of performance, they tend to set them lower than their boss (teacher) would. _____ (X)

   If people are allowed to set their own goals and standards of performance, they tend to set them higher than their boss (teacher) would. _____ (Y)

   Total 10

Add up your Theory X scores and Theory Y scores, and the higher one suggests your assumptions about people.

the discussion was about attitude toward leadership and not about the actual behaviour. Not only is there an immense gap between theory and practice, between what people say should happen and what they actually do, but different situations require different kinds of leadership.

The "bull sessions" may then move on to compare the various leadership styles, trying to determine the best one. Often the comparisons will be between a concern for getting the job done and a concern for the well-being of the people in the situation. While a mixture of the two usually emerges as the best style, there is not a high correlation between concerns and behaviour.

What really counts is not the attitudes and posturing about leadership but the actual behaviour and the results the behaviour has in the specific situation. We want to discourage the attention given to input variables (values, assumptions, attitudes, and concerns) and concentrate on the behaviour and its impact. This means we are looking at what happened as a result of the leadership intervention and how useful these results were. Loving the fourth grader who can't read is less effective than a directive program that quickly teaches new reading skills. Or rather than argue about the playing styles of the Maple Leafs' hockey team members, we want to look at their win/loss record and whether they won the Stanley Cup. Results are the task accomplishment and the impact on human resources. The Maple Leafs might win the Stanley Cup but lose three key players in the process. In assessing leadership behaviour it is helpful to look at *success*, which is accomplishment of the immediate goal, and at *effectiveness*, which is the longer-term effect on the group or organization. Talk about "preferred styles of leadership" blurs the issue. Concentrate on impact and results.

Leadership Summary

While leaders have some traits or characteristics that differentiate them from followers, these characteristics are not very important in understanding leadership and are usually related to the situation in which the leadership takes place. Leadership is best thought of as a group function where most members will be contributing to the achievement of group goals and to the maintenance and growth of the group. Depending on the situational factors, different styles of leadership or amounts of task achievement and group-building behaviours will be most appropriate. Diagnosing the quality of these situational factors can help to select the leadership style (or leader) most likely to be effective in that situation.[4] Leaders, regardless of gender, can increase their effectiveness by enlarging their repertoire of task and group-building skills, and by sharpening their diagnostic skills.

READER APPLICATIONS OF THESE UNDERSTANDINGS

1. As a member in a new group: talk a fair bit but not too much; memorize the names of the other members and use them as much as possible (you have to know the players to lead the team);

---

[4] Diagnostic tools and methods are presented in *How to Observe your Group*, one of nine books in this series.

and be hearty in your approbation and lavish in your praise (recognition and support).

2. As a new member in an old group: be relatively quiet and don't express any opinions until you have learned the group's usual way of doing things (values and traditions). Then show you accept these usual ways before introducing new ideas.

3. Decide if you want to contribute to managing the group or leading it or both. [Hedley often volunteers to be group recorder — second most powerful position — in order to use his influence more subtly.]

4. Try to balance your contribution to task accomplishment with support to individual members, mentioning a specific contribution they made to the group that you appreciate.

5. Be ready to try to mediate and negotiate "the least worst" (but still painful) decision/compromise that can be agreed to.[5]

6. While trying to increase the range and balance of your leadership styles is worthwhile, you will achieve more by assessing and diagnosing the maturity level of the group to know what leadership roles will be most effective.

---

[5] See *Leading and Managing Dynamic Groups* in the Dimock's series, p. 120ff, for 14 helpful techniques.

Group Structure

3

The section on leadership concluded that there were two major ways leaders could increase their effectiveness: enlarging their repertoire of task- and group-building behaviours and improving their group diagnostic skills. Countless studies on the outcomes of leadership training have not been encouraging. While it seems possible to help leaders develop additional task and group-building skills, this has had little impact on modifying the leaders' preferred or basic leadership style. Yet, in recent years there have been hundreds of leadership training programs and hardly a program on improving group diagnostic skills.

People who come together in groups tend to form structures and develop standards that help them to operate effectively and maintain themselves as a group. These standards or "usual ways of doing things" are most helpful to the group as everyone knows what is going to happen and how it is going to happen. These clear cut procedures or ways of doing things are evident in Parliament, business meetings, church services, charity programs, and nursing team report sessions. These "usual ways of doing things" are often called the culture of the group or organization. Members are expected to conform to these standards or informal rules and pressure is often exerted by the group on individuals who deviate from them.

3

From this process of social control a group derives its strength to pull together as a group and increase its effectiveness and morale.

A group or team is more than the sum of its parts — it is a social system with its own structure and culture. Once a structure and culture are established, they may be fairly difficult to change and studies have shown it is often easier to start up a new group than to get an existing group to change. Members may come and go in a group but as the culture belongs to the group as a whole, it stays put. Only by changing a "critical mass" of the members at one time is there a fair chance that the usual ways of doing things might also change.

There are two sources of norms and standards in most groups: those that originate from the organization (recreation centre, business, school, hospital, community agency) and those that are established informally by the group and individuals. A good example of external and internal norms at work can usually be found around meeting times or work hours. The external norm is that the meeting will start at 19:30 or the working day at 09:00, yet members usually know what time it will really start or when other people will arrive. In one organization with which I was associated, the work day started at 09:00 and people usually arrived about then but took fifteen or twenty minutes to get and drink coffee. In a sense they met the external norm by being on time yet the informal norm was that actual work started 20 to 30 minutes later. Groups rarely vote on which norms to adopt but rather gradually align their behaviours to match certain standards.

These norms mobilize powerful forces that influence the behaviour of members and determine the outcome of many organizational goals. Understanding and working with these norms can provide the essential element that is often missing in our work with groups, whether it be team teaching in education, coaching a team, leading a patient care planning team in a medical setting, or working on a community rehabilitation program. It is also these norms, along with the technical skills and competence of the members, that determine what will be the most effective leadership style for that group. And if changes are to be made in the way the group is working, it is these norms that will have to change.

GROUP MEMBERSHIP

All individuals have the same basic needs for approval, security, recognition, a sense of accomplishment, and power. Most of these needs, like other physical, educational, and spiritual needs in our society, are satisfied through relationships with other individuals or groups of individuals. Generally, people try to find relationships or groups in which these needs can be met. Individuals are attracted to groups that appear to be able to meet their needs; hence, in any group situation members are looking for ways to satisfy their needs. It is our experience that the two most prominent needs in a group are control and self-advancement.

Members who form a group on a voluntary basis, such as a team or club that meets after work, are more likely to find satisfaction and be attracted to the group than members who are not free to come and go, such as in a school class or work unit. Dimock's father found in his studies that voluntary groups had more solidarity and influence on member behaviour than groups with non-voluntary members. Procedures or activities that increase the satisfaction of member needs usually increase the group's solidarity too.

The specific attraction to a particular group may be based on personal attraction to the other members, monetary return, the nature of the group goals or tasks, or the prestige of the group in the eyes of other people. A person may find satisfaction in a group because the members like her serious generation studies and make her feel secure. Or, the activity of the group such as a team sport, singing, craft work, or skiing may provide an opportunity for her to gain considerable recognition if she excels in that skill. A group taking on worthwhile community service projects can provide a real sense of accomplishment for its members. Sometimes people seek membership in a group that has high prestige in the community, hoping it will give them more acceptance or perhaps open up contacts for furthering business and professional interests. And, of course, groups that can or might provide large amounts of money are winners for that kind of self-advancement.

Physical location is another factor affecting attraction to a group and membership. Early Studies of Y's and Boys' and Girls' Clubs showed that most members came from within a mile radius of the building. Joining a group now is related to what is offered at a convenient location with suitable parking. Informal groups in the community such as bridge clubs and Sunday hockey players tend to be composed of people who live close to one another. Also in work situations informal groups often reflect the physical proximity of the members.

Recognizing the reasons members join a group and then helping to satisfy these reasons is a powerful way of building strong, healthy groups. Probably the most common misconception in this regard is leaders who assume members have joined their groups because of the content of their activity such as a book review club, soccer team, ceramics group, or Shakespeare class. In reality, members often join for social reasons and the activity simply provides a vehicle and legitimization for getting together to meet the individual's needs.

Summing up the membership in a group and having some understanding of members' motivation, if any, for being in the group, keep in mind the likely two parts. There are the usual reasons for being in the group related to the purpose and activity of the group: to learn a foreign language; to become a nurse; to play hockey and get exercise. But once members are in the group, their more personal motivations will emerge and influence the operation of the group. An informal study of an English class in a university's night school revealed, on probing, that half the class were there to meet other students with dating them in mind. Thus, straight lectures were received nonchalantly while small-group assignments were winners.

The most useful place to start in making some assumptions about members' unmentionable motivations is with those that are most likely — control and self-advancement. Our key word for remembering basic human needs is REAPS. This stands for Recognition, Experience, Approval, Power, and Security. Power and control usually top the list as people like to have their own way and have other people behave and do what they would like them to. Power and control also means that they will likely get the attention, approval, and recognition they desire. Plus they can feel more secure in situations that they control as there will be few surprises to upset them.

Self-advancement can include more of the same things on the control list such as more recognition and approval, more money or organization advancement such as promotions, awards, or bonuses. In a nutshell, self-advancement is the desire for more of anything or everything — sometimes just because it is there. The greed may be for material things — electronic gadgets, trips, fast cars, stylish clothes, or money — but it can also be for more friends, approval, and recognition, perhaps especially from the opposite sex.

Many group dynamics can best be understood by asking yourself whether the argument or problem solving discussion that's going nowhere can be explained as a control issue or a self-advancement ploy. Dimock started this idea of checking the process (hidden agenda) when the content didn't make sense to him while working in the Montreal

Children's Hospital. Two six-year-olds were fighting for possession of a tricycle — yes, Dimock introduced them over the objection of the chief physician who, when he complained to the director, was told to just open his legs and let the kids drive through. Dimock, in his conflict solving mode, quickly produced an exactly similar tricycle, only to find they continued to struggle over the first one. Since then he has found that over half of the conflicts he has managed have little or nothing to do with the subject matter and everything to do with winning the control issue.

FACTORS CONTRIBUTING TO STRONG GROUPS

The strength or solidarity of a group is determined chiefly by the personal need or desire for satisfaction it provides members or by the expectation of that need for satisfaction. Solidarity and cohesion increase as the group becomes more attractive to the members and there is an increased interest in taking part in its programs. The more that members are attracted to a group because of what it can or does offer them, the higher will be its cohesion. An individual who is lured to a group on the promise of exciting activities and personal rewards will not continue to be attracted to the group if it does not live up to expectations or in other ways provide personal satisfaction. The basis of a group's solidarity often determines how members will react in a group. If the basis of attraction to the group is the personal relations with other members, then meetings are likely to be warm and friendly with perhaps only moderate interest in planning and decision making related to tasks. This appeared to be the case in the study of a community development project a few years ago where the core planning group were young homemakers who enjoyed their personal relations. Although interested in the community project, it was not the basis of attraction to the group. The formal planning session with a chairperson, agenda, and minutes did not meet the group's needs and we instituted an unstructured meeting after the formal meeting where people talked about what they were feeling during the meeting or about what was going on in their lives.

Another factor contributing to group strength is the size of the group: other things being equal, smaller groups are more cohesive than larger groups. In a small group (5–13 members) there is more interaction among members and increased interaction tends to increase positive feelings among members which, in turn, increases attraction for the group. And, the increased participation possible in a small group for each member also promotes satisfaction. Geographical location and physical proximity also tend to increase interaction and thus can be another contributor to group strength.

Leadership style has a considerable impact on solidarity with facilitating, participative-oriented leadership encouraging interaction and relationship building. Certainly, the more that members participating in making the decisions that affect them have a clear picture of the goals of the group and have a recognized part to play in helping the group reach those goals, the higher will be the group's cohesion. Coaching and facilitative leaders also help members get recognition and self-enhancement as the group goes about its work and this increases attraction to the group. Showing concern for members' well-being is consistently related to group cohesion. Task-oriented styles can contribute to group strength by increasing satisfaction with concrete accomplishments and especially by helping members clarify their expectations of the group. Permissive and "laissez-faire" styles have no pattern of relationship to group cohesion.

We have observed in classrooms where students are assigned to groups on an arbitrary basis a wide variance in performance. In some groups members pull together to achieve their goals and have fun and personal satisfaction in the process, whereas in other groups the members argue constantly and appear to meet their individual needs at the expense of the group. The frustration and low grade for the group's task influences members to dislike the group experience and probably the course. Over the years we've learned that giving the groups more coaching in becoming a strong group has paid off in students' satisfaction and course achievement. We have reduced group size, provided materials on working in groups, let the students select the other members of their group, and arranged group-building exercises for all the groups.

Groups where members are working toward a common goal on a cooperative basis are usually more cohesive than groups in which the members are in competition with one another. Competition with an outside group, however, can have a powerful influence in strengthening a group's solidarity. This understanding is frequently used by sales managers, team leaders, school teachers, and even government as they seek an outside group to "fight" against, expecting the competition to pull the group together and increase task accomplishment in the process. While competition does tend to increase cohesion, it is not without detriment to the group as leadership usually centralizes and becomes more directive, tension rises, and aggression and scapegoating increase.

Working with an outside group on a vital task that requires the full participation of members of both groups is about as powerful an influence on cohesion as competition. This approach also increases cohesion without harmful side effects on the group. Interest in win-win games, activities, and projects has demonstrated useful alternatives to traditional win-lose activities and the swing in its direction will increase as the range and quality of activities continue to expand.

Anything that helps a group to feel special or unique can contribute to group strength such as a name, insignia, pennant, special meeting room, unique stationery, initiation rituals, and regular ceremonies. Many groups have special songs or cheers that add to group spirit. In Japan and a few North American companies, some workgroups start the day with a company song followed by a traditional set of physical exercises. Probably the biggest winner along this line is some sort of distinguishing costume. IBM has its three-piece suits and white shirts; youth groups have their jeans and jogging shoes; and street gangs, their "all the same" jackets, hats, or hairstyles. Organizations can also contribute to the solidarity of their groups by playing up their importance to the community, the kind of public support and financial assistance they receive (or give), their national or international status, and anything else that might increase their groups' attractiveness.

There is some support for the assumption that the difficulty of getting into a group increases its attraction for members. People often want most of those things which are hard to get while easy things are taken for granted. If people work hard to qualify for group membership, it is expected that they will value that membership more highly than otherwise. Asking too little of group members loses more members than asking for a high, but attainable, contribution.

New groups usually set very high and quite optimistic goals, and groups that are working toward a clear set of overall goals tend to prefer more difficult short-term goals to easy ones. Group goals can be increased after both success and failure and may become unattainable. The frustration and disappointment this can generate may reduce the group's attractiveness and thus its cohesion. High but attainable goals are encouraged by frequent reports on results to provide comparisons and a realistic basis for setting new goals.

Cohesion is the glue that holds groups together, and if factors inside or outside the group start to decrease this cohesion, the group will begin to fall apart. If action is not taken to reverse this trend, there will be disorganization and collapse, and if the group is a voluntary one, the members will go their separate ways. Members will leave a voluntary group at the point where the forces attracting them to the group are equal to, or outnumbered by, the forces pulling them away from the group. We might say that when the net attractiveness of a group is zero or a negative amount, its members will start leaving. While attractiveness dimensions vary from member to member, the net attractiveness is often similar and when this point is reached, usually several members will leave at the same time (especially if part of their attraction was to each other). A high turnover in membership is usually a pretty accurate symptom of an unhealthy group. Some groups with poor group strength can be lost for several years with the members in an apathetic state simply because the groups have become institutionalized and the members continue to come as part of a routine or memories of other days.

As we review the new realities described in Part One there are several of them that directly affect the cohesion of a group — the glue that holds it together and enables it to work collaboratively. In brief, they are: the digital revolution; increasing numbers of female and multicultural members; demographics including age, language, and culture; our sensitivities to our pluralistic society; and financial pressures on workgroups. If "birds of a feather flock together", we have more kinds of "birds" to integrate into our workgroups if they are going to fly together. The digital revolution is owned and operated by young folks and the older, "senior" members tend to resist the technology and their taking control of the group. Many more work teams now have a female supervisor and female members often outnumber males. Add the increasing number of multicultural members who may have different perceptions and beliefs about the role of women to the list of issues to be integrated to build group cohesion. Now throw in the focused literacy of possible members with English as a second language who are fluent verbally, can twitter a bit, but would have a tough time reading this book. Add to it the financial restraints on staff development and training (usually the first department to be cut) and no time and resources to build a cohesive group seriously impact the creation and growth of a group. We will develop this important basic group dimension further as we go along.

In summing up we'd like to highlight that for a group to be strong, members must be attracted to the group, be clear about their role in the group and how they can contribute to achieving the group's goals, and integrate the group's standards and norms. Groups function most effectively when members agree on goals, standards, and usual ways of doing things. These, in turn, help all the members to know what is expected of them, how they can behave most appropriately and get recognition and approval, what they can expect from their colleagues, and how the group is likely to meet their personal and professional needs. In a cohesive group, members want their group to succeed so they can continue to find the satisfactions that attracted them to the group, and as it continues to succeed members glow with pride and satisfaction about their efforts. An identity and recognition as a separate group — high but attainable goals, optimal interaction and proximity — and facilitative leadership that encourages participation in decision making and member well-being help build a cohesive group. The new realities of the previous paragraph suggest that some groups may not be able to achieve this desired level of cohesiveness and are open to different ways of accomplishing their tasks.

GROUP STANDARDS AND SOCIAL CONTROL

The cohesion of a group is the glue that holds it together and makes it click. Cohesion — the sum of members' attraction to the group — provides the power to motivate members to abide by a group's standards and usual ways of working. Without solidarity there is little group influence over members' behaviour and unless the group has some coercive power available (such as in schools and many work places), the group can end up a collection of individuals all doing their own things. As a group develops standards about what is acceptable member behaviour, it also develops forces which put pressure on members to conform to these standards. The more members are attracted to the group and want to see it succeed, the stronger the forces are likely to be. An understanding of group standards and the forces supporting them can help to explain what is going on in a group and why some groups are successful and some are not. Guiding these forces can be an important contribution of the group leader to the value of the experience for the members.

Healthy groups encourage the *conformity* of members to group standards but this does not mean *uniformity of behaviour*. Standards of healthy groups may encourage all members to make their unique contributions to the group — that is, people should be themselves as much as possible. Alternately, the expectations for participants may be that they will work in cooperative, interdependent ways; participate in consensual decision-making processes; and express any differences they feel so the group can consider all alternatives. In these groups, individuals who think and feel differently from the group (the creative minority) are supported by the group's standards for their differences as long as they also conform to working in cooperative, interdependent ways around the differences. Having members conform by expressing similar opinions or all acting the same does not usually help a group. But having members conform to a standard of sticking together to try to work out differences, to find decisions that will be tolerable to all, is most desirable.

Uniformity of behaviour where members are expected to think, dress and act alike is usually found in groups that are immature, anxious, or frightened, or under considerable pressure from outside the group. We see these uniformity groups in military boot camps, street gangs, and religious cults. To these groups with their insecure members, having everyone "talk the same" appears to protect the group against these fears. While the *uniformity* and "sheep-like" behaviour of members is a real concern in a freedom-loving, humanistic society, it is usually a symptom of scared, pressured, or immature groups. Helping to develop strong, healthy groups reduces the need for restrictive group standards based on uniformity of behaviour. Let's put our energies into working on the problem, not railing about the symptoms.

The function of social pressures on members to conform to group standards is to help facilitate and organize the accomplishment of group goals and maintain the group as a functioning social system. To have a successful meeting, for instance, a group needs most of its members to be there and at about the same time (or the ones who come early may get frustrated and leave). Some kind of a standard with some pressure to abide by the standard is useful to group members. The pressure can take the form of a "you're late again" comment, a fine, an extra duty, and all the way up to a dismissal from the group. Some time ago a news story appeared about a high school basketball team that was hell-bent on winning all its games and set up rigid rules for training and practice which were strictly enforced. Players breaking the ten o'clock curfew were brought before the team and "pressured" back into line. Missing practice or breaking curfew more than once could result in being expelled from the team. This aspect of social pressure seems to be well summarized in the saying "to get along, you go along".

The more members are attracted to a group, or need the job, and internalize its goals, the more likely they are to abide by the group's standards and pressure others to do the same. This social control helps the group to work expediently and greatly increases the satisfaction of participants with the group. This, in turn, helps to increase the group's solidarity. It is a circular phenomenon as the more cohesive a group is, the more it can exert social pressure; the more it can exert pressure in members to conform to its standards, the greater will be the members' satisfaction; and the greater the satisfaction of members with the group, the higher will be its cohesion.

The Power of Group Pressure

The power of group pressure has been frequently illustrated in laboratory experiments where individuals were pressured by others into an opinion or behaviour which was against their better judgment. In one classical study a naive subject was shown a small ray of light in a dark room and asked to estimate the distance of its movement. It was very difficult to tell if the light was moving or not as there were no reference points, but when a person was joined by others who were in on the experiment and pretended they saw the light moving (it did not move), the naive subject started making similar estimates. Most subjects were heavily influenced by the other members' opinions.

In another study subjects were asked to match the length of a standard line with three comparison lines (**Figure 7**). The three comparison lines were of quite different length and it was easy to tell which lines matched. In order to study the effect on the subjects of majority opinions which appeared contrary to fact, seven other people who were "in cahoots" with the experimenter were added to form a group. These members gave incorrect answers and most subjects when confronted by the incorrect group majority opinion modified their own judgments. About a third of the subjects distorted their judgments in order to completely agree with the majority.

Another "shocking" experiment went even further in studying conformity to authority. The above studies had suggested that if one of the group members "in cahoots" with the experimenter had some authority status, the naive subject was more likely to accept that person's judgment than other group members. So in this experiment the naive

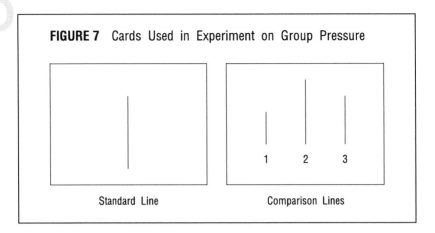

FIGURE 7 Cards Used in Experiment on Group Pressure

Standard Line

Comparison Lines

1   2   3

subject was directed to administer an electric shock to a victim under the guise of a study of the effects of punishment on memory. Over half of the subjects, on the direction of the experimenter, administered "dangerous, severe shocks" to the victims (though the victims yelled and screamed on being shocked, it was all faked). This power of the authority figure was greatly over-estimated by the research team.

Subjects were more likely to conform to group pressure in the first study where the ray of light presented a vague or ambiguous stimulus than in the second study where the lines had clear parameters. It may be concluded that the more general or ambiguous the topic of discussion, the more an individual will be influenced by majority opinions. In a group setting, a member will more likely conform to group pressure when discussing what life will be like 10 years from now than when discussing the legal status of capital punishment.

THE IMPACT OF GROUP PRESSURE

The more participants want to or need to remain in a group the more likely they are to abide by its standards. The more members value the standard, see its usefulness, and believe that adhering to that standard will help the group, the more they will support it and pressure other members to do so. A person who deviates from the norms of the group gradually becomes the focus of attention. At first she may be ignored and have nothing said about her conduct, but as that doesn't give a very clear message the deviant may miss it completely. This is the typical "cold shoulder" treatment. Similar behaviour within a short time span may bring members to talk about her behind her back, hoping that the word will get back to her. The next level is usually some kind of side remark said in the person's presence but in a jocular manner. The deviant continues to be isolated from other communication to strengthen the rejection, and additional bad-mouthing bringing up other faults helps to increase the isolation. The final form of group pressure is some kind of direct confrontation by the group, or by a member or two who take on the role of group enforcer. Some kind of separation or removal from the group may be threatened at that time. In addition to actual removal, a group may withdraw the deviant's privileges (take away a parking space, move her to a smaller office, take back loaned equipment), give her dead-end assignments, send her on "wild goose chases", and cut her off from notification of future meetings and other important communication.

How a deviant will respond to group pressure depends not only on how much he wants to stay in the group, but on how important continuing that behaviour is to him. It also depends on how clear and harsh the messages and punishments are as he may be able to tolerate the snide remarks, but find a conspiracy of silence too much to handle. Sometimes a behaviour that is found deviant in one group is the accepted standard in another and the individual is faced with conflicting values. In such cases he will usually stick with the behaviour approved by the group that is most attractive to him. Parents are shocked when their children continue behaviour that is supported in their peer group of age-mates but is in defiance of family standards and parental pressure to conform. Occasionally for some young people, it is more important to have the acceptance of their age-mates than that of their parents.

People are more likely to conform to a group's standards if it is the most important group in their life, or if, at least for a period of time, it is the only group. Without outside reference points and reminders of usual standards, the power of the present group increases immensely. The armed forces use this technique in virtually isolating new recruits in boot camp. Hospitals do the same when they limit or otherwise discourage outsiders from visiting as this increases the adherence of patients to hospital norms. Similar strong pressures develop in communes, monasteries, submarines, prisons, and isolated oil rigs or work areas.

This factor has been used in training programs that were trying to increase the impact of the training on group participants.

3

Personal growth groups may be held on a residential basis in a remote area. Non-participants (family members or friends) are not allowed and telephones are not readily available (no calls are taken during work sessions). Most activities — eating, sleeping, recreation — are done with other members, thus increasing interaction and group influence potential. Some treatment groups intensify this process by meeting for 18 or 20 hours a day non-stop and then perhaps sleeping in the same room. It is well documented how powerful this isolation from usual activities and reference points can be and how, after a few days, participants are ready to experiment with very new and different behaviour. Group leaders work at building group standards that will encourage this freeing up, self-exploration process by setting up group rules, modelling appropriate behaviour, and rewarding and perhaps punishing those who do and don't conform to the standards.

These are powerful forces that have a significant impact on attitude and behaviour change, and while the participants of personal growth groups are paying big money for the opportunity, the same factors make up the pressures used in "brainwashing" where the procedures are not voluntarily accepted by the captive and often coerced participants (see **Figures 8** and **9**).

FIGURE 8 Factors Affecting the Strength of Group Pressures

1. **The effect conformity will have on group success:** Deviant behaviour blocking the group from an important objective will receive more pressure than deviation which is merely annoying and distracting.

2. **The cohesion of the group:** Cohesive groups have more power to exert strong pressures, and are more likely to use them.

3. **Discrepancy of deviant behaviour:** The wider the divergence of behaviour from accepted standards, the greater will be the pressure to conform.

4. **Group status of the deviant:** Members who are well accepted by the group and are moving up in the system will receive more pressure than "odd balls" who aren't important to the group.

5. **Visibility of the deviation:** High visibility deviations such as dress, public statements, and written documents receive more pressure than washroom mutterings.

FIGURE 9 Factors Affecting Conformity to Pressures

1. **Desire or need to remain part of the group:** The more a member sees the group as attractive and wants to retain membership, the greater will be the influence of group pressures toward conformity.

2. **The strength, visibility, and clarity of pressures:** Public humiliation with a comprehensive review of transgressions is more powerful than a few vague, snarky comments in the parking lot.

3. **Conflicts with other group standards:** If conforming to the standards of one group means breaking the standards of an equally important group in a way that is highly visible, it will be less acceptable than if there is no conflict.

4. **The character of the individual:** Individuals vary in their proneness to yield to group pressure because of personal factors. People with self-confidence and inner security are least likely to be affected by social pressure.

5. **The certainty of the sanctions:** Group pressure that leaves no doubt about what will happen as a result of the deviant behaviour is most likely to be effective.

Many everyday groups in social agencies, business, churches, and schools use some of these factors when they go on a trip together or attend a conference, hold meetings off the job site, go on a retreat, or just schedule in a weekend for intensive work on a particular problem. Increasing physical togetherness, interaction, and isolation can help to maximize the impact of pressures toward group standards.

Groups that are strong and healthy encourage members to think and act creatively, initiate new ideas, and propose different ways of doing things. This allows some deviation from usual ways of doing things and will be tolerated, or even encouraged, if the deviant is a high status member of the group and the behaviour holds some hope of being useful to the group. At other times minor infractions of group standards by well-accepted members may be tolerated as others say "there goes Marilyn again, pushing for her special project." Members also earn the right to be different, based on their past contribution to the group. If new members complain about their idiosyncrasy, they are told of their previous outstanding services to the group.

3

Conformity

Women conform more than men, although it seems to be only in face-to-face situations. For centuries, American juries didn't include women because it was argued that women couldn't influence others or hold to their own private views so they couldn't contribute to the decision. A number of factors have been identified that combine to create this sex difference in conformity. In some cultures women are encouraged to adopt a feminine sex role that includes such characteristics as reliance on others, submissiveness, and a tendency to yield to the decisions of others. Men, in contrast, are taught to be independent, unemotional, and assertive. When women find themselves in a conformity situation, they tend to yield to the majority while men in those types of situations aggressively defend their viewpoints. Evidence also indicates that women and men who adopt a feminine sex role conform more than women and men who adopt a masculine role or an androgynous sex-role orientation. Interpersonal forces also contribute to the sex difference in conformity. Women, more than men, tend to agree with fellow group members to maintain group harmony while men disagree with others to create the impression of independence and to gain power. A number of studies suggest that women, in contrast to men, vary their expressed opinions in order to match the views of attractive male partners, use opinion conformity as a self-presentational tactic, and interpret conformity as a sign of competence rather than weakness. Since sex roles have changed in many cultures in recent years, sex differences in conformity rates, too, have become less evident which indicates that socialization and culture, rather than sex, influences conformity.

Group Structure and Goals

The presentation on group structure, so far, has discussed group membership and what attracts people to groups — factors related to group solidarity and group standards and social control. To continue the presentation of group standards and norms, it is helpful to look at the kind of goals a group has and how the members interact and make decisions. These dimensions help to round out a picture of a group and provide a fairly comprehensive overview of group structure (Climate, Involvement, Interaction, Cohesion, and Productivity).

Group goals can be rated on the extent to which they encourage members to work together and collaborate, work independently, or compete. Members of boards of directors of the community serving associations with whom we've worked usually see themselves working toward a common goal and collaboration as helping to achieve their goals. But when Dimock was a member of a swimming team, members worked toward a common goal (being conference champions) though winning depended on the skills of individual members. As a consultant to a large insurance company, Dimock found the salespeople and managers in competition with one another over the dollar volume of sales. The differences in these goals typically influence group structure. Groups with goals achieved through collaboration develop standards related to the quality of the group's performance. Members become more concerned about what happens to the group's performance than about their own performance. This often results in more cohesion, more interaction, and more pressures for members to conform to group standards. And if the members participated in establishing the group's goal, their commitment to it and readiness to abide by group standards and to encourage others to do so increase. This increased motivation for group success and thus the attractiveness of the group builds group solidarity. And as members' desire for group success increases so do efforts to achieve that success.

For example, a student group assigned a specific topic or case to analyze and report on will usually have less motivation than a team that has selected its own topic or case. This is also true of a team of nurses on a ward where patients, charting, and other tasks may be assigned rather than being based on group decisions. It is back to our rule that, as much as is practical, "decisions should be made by the people affected by them."

During an extensive study of over a thousand recreation workers (Dimock, 1979), it was found that there were two types of groups the recreation workers led: goals achieved through member collaboration groups; and goals achieved through individual successes groups. In the latter category were figure skating, swimming, skiing, gymnastics, squash, and similar individual sport or activity groups. The relationships of the members in the groups were different and, in individual activity groups, the staff used coaching styles of leadership while in the other groups the facilitating style was more appropriate. The concept of superordinate goals is that when the goals can only be accomplished by all the members of one or more groups working together, it becomes a powerful unifying force. Group motivation is most likely to develop when the group's accomplishments can be attributed to the effort of the group as a whole rather than to individual members.

Status and Position (Hierarchical Structures)

Norms and structure provide order for the group and help to coordinate and focus individual behaviour. Knowing who gets to do what, and what the expectations are for each member is an important part of a group working smoothly, with a high level of satisfaction for the members. To help clarify structure, groups develop a status or position hierarchy. The position hierarchy is based on assigned positions such as president, supervisor, team leader, chairperson, and may or may not be related to competence and popularity. But these positions are clearly visible and usually the power, privileges, and responsibilities that go with the position are pretty well defined.

There is another equally important hierarchy that is based on personal status and although it is rarely discussed, it exists in a definite form. Personal status is what people earn in their relationships with others and in their skills and abilities to help the group with its products. A street gang may base its status hierarchy on toughness; a board of directors, on financial resources; and a workgroup, on concern for others. More usually, there are a variety of factors determining to whom a group will assign personal status.

In the rural area we call this hierarchy a "gate order" as it describes cows coming into the barn from the field. As milking time approaches the cows bunch up at the gate, blocking the entrance into the barn. Once the gate is opened the cows file quickly through and always in the same gate order. Imagine the confusion and shoving if the cows did not know what the gate order was and where their position occurred. Chickens have the same behaviour at feeding time and we call this a pecking order.

The status hierarchy in groups of people performs much the same function of organization and coordination. However, as humans don't "line up" and demonstrate the order as clearly as cows, people have to refine their observation skills to pick it up. Groups with clearly established hierarchies — where all participants know what is expected of them and what they can expect from each other — function more satisfactorily than groups where the hierarchy remains vague. In new groups much of the early activity can be best understood as members are trying to work out their hierarchy and are "jockeying for position" in the process. Accuracy in perceiving the status positions of others is closely associated with status as the members who can't put it together usually don't know what is going on in the group or where they stand with other people and this decreases their usefulness and prestige.

Hierarchical structures have been developing and refining themselves everywhere since recorded history. The clarity of the "pecking order", and its effectiveness, has been a key dimension of the success of various societies since the Egyptians and Romans. The criteria for creating the order has changed from the family into which you were born — royalty, common person, servant, or indentured worker, serf or alone — to profession, wealth, education, and perhaps glamour. Each criteria has its own order of importance with rankings of the country's richest people, professions (doctors and professors near the top and used car salespeople at the bottom), education (with Harvard, Yale, and Columbia at the top in the United States, McGill and the University of Toronto in Canada), and so on. This is described to illustrate the solid foundation of hierarchies and their importance in our society. It also helps to understand why power and control are chief personal motivators and therefore important to understand and utilize in "making workgroups effective".

Influence and Status

Studies of the emergence of leaders in small, unstructured discussion groups tend to find men outnumbering women in the leadership role. In several studies of mixed gender groups, women displayed fewer leadership actions than men and both leaders and followers perceived the female leaders to be less dominant than male leaders. There is also evidence that a lone man in an all-female group often becomes the leader whereas a lone female in an otherwise all-male group has little influence. There seems to be a tendency for men to dominate women in informal discussion groups, even when the women and men are all deemed to be androgynous. Several studies suggest that even women who are interpersonally dominant cannot escape the constraints of this gender bias. However, when groups are warned beforehand about the tendency to favour men, women and men share leadership equally.

Women are often accorded less status than men in groups. Although initially, group members may start off on an equal footing, over time, status differentiation (where certain individuals acquire the authority to coordinate the group's activities and provide others with guidance) usually takes place.

Despite attitudinal changes in sexist and racist attitudes in society, stereotypical biases still make gaining status in small groups a difficult task for women and minorities. Women report dissatisfaction with their unfairly low status rankings, and often the rest of the group is uncertain about their status. Group performance, too, can suffer as the group overlooks the valuable contributions offered by members who are competent but not considered worthy of high status. Biases in status allocations can be overcome over time as women demonstrate their abilities at the group tasks. It seems that women have to put extra effort into their activities just to remain on par with men. Women can also gain status in groups if they act in group-oriented ways rather than in a self-oriented manner. One study trained males and females to adopt either a cooperative, friendly interaction style or an emotionally distant, self-absorbed style. Men in all-female groups achieved high status no matter what style they exhibited, but the women in all-male groups achieved high status only if they displayed a group-oriented motivation. The same kinds of biases can affect single parents, physically handi-capped persons, young or old age groups, and people from a specific city.

Decision-Making Structures

Closely related to the question of who has power in the group, as illus-trated by a status hierarchy, is the question of "who gets to decide what for whom". There are two parts to this question that are important to the group as both of them affect cohesion and member satisfaction. First, we should check on how clear and consistent the deciding pro-cesses are, for the clearer they are the greater will be their potential usefulness. Second, the procedures used will also influence cohesion and motivation as the more the number of members join in establishing group goals, and see them as appropriate and attainable, the higher will be the cohesion and member readiness to work on these goals.

The clarity of the structure, irrespective of how appropriate the structure is to the needs of the group, is important. Structures that are clear can be changed while it is much harder to deal with vague struc-tures. Some leaders and managers seem to recognize this intuitively and keep the structures vague and constantly changing so as to retain their power and control by avoiding input or confrontation from others. Structures that become too specific can be very restrictive and we are sure that "Robert's Rules of Order" have hindered as many groups as they have helped. Inconsistencies in structures or procedures are extremely frustrating and many is the time we have heard children, stu-dents and workers say "if only they would be consistent I wouldn't mind so much what they *did*." Ideally we would choose norms and structures that continually develop and evolve through the participation of group members so that they can make the optimal contributions to the group but that are always clear to members.

Frequently Asked Questions

A frequently asked and extensively studied question is "does increasing cohesion increase productivity?" The book is still open on this question as it does not appear that there is any consistent pattern. It is clear, however, that increasing cohesion increases member satisfaction with the group. But this is not a big surprise as cohesion is defined as the sum of members' attraction to the group.

"Are individuals or groups more effective in accomplishing tasks?" This has probably been one of the most frequently conducted experiments and yet the results seem to be related to the type of task selected for the study. In any case, it is a non-issue for practitioners as the question isn't "is this a task for an individual or for a group?" but "how can I motivate people to do this task and help them gain satisfaction in the process?" The earliest studies were done by educators trying to determine if homework was done best individually or in groups. These days, with the competition from other areas for students' time and an awareness that some people work better together and some alone, we want to use whatever approach will motivate students to do any homework and that there might have been a better way under laboratory conditions has little relation to our goal. This is especially the case for the digital generation.

As leaders become aware of the concepts and applications described in this and similar publications and see how they can help them achieve their goals with groups, they ask "But if I use my understanding of group dynamics aren't I manipulating the group?" All leadership acts or interventions are manipulations in that they are attempts to move the group in some direction related to task accomplishment or group maintenance. Being aware of what is going on in a group and what the likely outcomes of various acts might be increases their influence. Manipulation is defined as "skilful or dexterous management" — an appropriate goal for group leaders. The greater concern is likely whether or not the acts are being used in a deceptive way against the best interests of others. Straightforward interventions by a leader are unlikely to be influential if they are against the best interests of the group because the group is stronger than the leader. Also leaders are unable to get a group to accept their goals until they have gained high prestige status by accepting and working toward the goals of the group. Only coercion or some source of strong control makes it possible to move a group toward ends that the group does not accept. Yet even prison riots have been successful in getting the warden fired.

Social Control and Individual Development

Many of the goals of human service workers and managers are related to helping people learn, grow, and become more fully functioning as individuals. Providing information that will change behaviour, teach new skills, or try to reverse self-defeating attitudes occupies much time and effort. The concepts outlined in this section indicate that much of an individual's behaviour is tied up with the norms of the groups to which that person belongs. The new approach that has been consistently developing alongside these insights is that individual behaviour can be influenced most effectively by working through the norms and standards of the groups to which the individual belongs. As the group with its norms and standards has become the target for change in the human service, educational, treatment, and retraining programs, working with individuals in isolation from their reference groups has been on the wane.

Everywhere we look people are taking charge of their own lives. People generally do not see themselves as responsible for their problems, but they increasingly see themselves responsible for the solution. Sometimes taking responsibility for the solution means implementing the solution program themselves. For example, it's estimated that one-third of the population of North America in the mid-1990s was into alternative medicine. Every large city had a host of self-help groups where the participants helped each other with the illness or problem they shared. The groups were all organized and conducted by the participants with little or no professional help and usually with no institutional relationship. This was a significant change from earlier years where hospitals, social and health agencies, and mental health centres had control of all of the health care programs.

Often, however, taking responsibility for the solution means organizing a special interest group to demand the solution or compensation for the alleged wrong. The 1960s to 1980s had the flower children, or hippy generation, and the I-me and me-now generations; the 1990s was the era of victims, and the 2000s was the era of social action groups who often use aggressive action. Increasing numbers of people see themselves (or are taught to see themselves) as victims of something. They have been abused as a child, spouse, parent or employee (de-hired); neglected in some way or discriminated against because of their gender, sexual orientation, race, ethnic group, language, religion, occupation, geographical location, colour, or physical appearance. Others are physically, emotionally, mentally, or educationally handicapped, or in some other way disadvantaged — perhaps by a historical wrong 50 or 200 years ago.

These lobby, advocacy, or pressure groups have forever shifted the virtual monopoly held by institutions, governments, and their adherents (professionals, politicians, and bureaucrats) to the empowered groups of people taking charge of the issues and changing the norms, values, and traditions of society. As a result there are new coalitions of clients and professionals in the human services and community groups, such as parents taking over budgeting and personnel decisions for their schools, business and government radicalizing their organizational culture — their usual ways of doing things — and green groups organizing action on climate change.

Understanding Individuals in Groups

4

Understanding group behaviour is advanced by having some knowledge of the importance of groups in social development, an awareness of the personality characteristics individuals bring with them to groups, and an understanding of the similarities and differences among them. Almost all of the emotional and social needs of individuals find their satisfaction in relationships with others. Individuals moving into a new group experience bring the influence of previous group experiences, and typical modes of behaviour are recognized. Many phenomena in groups are products of the members interacting and are unique to that situation. They cannot be explained by just looking at the behaviour of individual members, for a group is more than the sum of its parts. Professional staff with their background in psychology and guidance can recognize and appreciate much of the behaviour they find in a group. Experience helps them to gain further understanding and enables them to make some assumptions about the reason for individual behaviour. But, they must be careful not to judge, and should assess motives in only a most cautious way. These professionals have a serious responsibility to help the workers they supervise, who have less training, and to recognize their limitations in doing any behaviour analysis or in playing armchair psychologist.

EMOTIONAL NEEDS AND BEHAVIOUR PATTERNS

Emotional needs have been categorized in different ways but usually include love, affection, security, recognition, a sense of belonging, and a feeling of self-worth. All of these needs find their fulfillment in relations with other people and there can be no affection or recognition without these other people. During a child's early years it is the family who provides most of the needs satisfaction, but as a child grows older, friends at school and at play become increasingly important in satisfying needs. And, as mentioned earlier, starting about age 11 and lasting through the teens, the attraction to age-mate groups because of their potential to satisfy these needs may exceed attraction to family.

All behaviour has some purpose or goal — people don't just "do things". If everything people do has some objective — some pay-off — it helps to look for the pay-off in trying to understand members' behaviour. Motivation for behaviour may be seen as partly unconscious with roots in early childhood. People may not know why they are doing certain things and perhaps ask others "why did I do that?" Yet the focus for group practitioners is not just in trying to understand why participants think they do certain things, but recognizing what they are getting out of their behaviour — what needs are being satisfied. Regulating increases and decreases in needs satisfaction may then influence behaviour.

Personality and behaviour patterns are developed from inherited potentialities and life experiences. The goal of these behaviour patterns is to provide physical security and satisfy physiological and emotional needs. As children are growing up, they find certain ways of finding satisfaction more successful than others. The behaviour that is most successful tends to be continued and over a period of time develops into a usual way of doing things.

These usual ways of doing things or behaviour patterns tend to develop fairly early in life and remain fairly stable thereafter. It is important that these behaviour patterns remain fairly stable as they provide security and equilibrium. Consequently, healthy individuals have a built-in resistance to making major changes in these patterns. People have a great potential for learning and personal growth, especially within the parameters of their behaviour patterns. Major changes in these basic patterns take place very slowly and usually with considerable effort, if at all.

GROWTH AND DEVELOPMENT

A useful framework for observing, understanding, and talking to others about individuals and groups is built around Schutz's three interpersonal relations orientations of *inclusion*, *control*, and *intimacy*. (See *How to Observe Your Group* for group applications and details.) All people are seen as having these three basic needs, which start developing in early childhood with inclusion as the first need to achieve. The achievement of the developmental need in the second stage of growth (control) is partly dependent on the successful accomplishment of the previous need. While a certain level of inclusion and control behaviour is developed in the first two years, there are further developments throughout life, but a child who has not developed behaviour skills to meet these needs in early childhood is handicapped in further development throughout life.

Inclusion

Inclusion can be described as the need to establish and maintain satisfactory relations with other people. This is a need for belonging, to be wanted by other people and in turn to be interested in them. The first year is a crucial time for the development of this sense of inclusion or belonging — of being wanted by one's parents and responding to their attention and care. Between four and six months of age, hungry babies will grow quiet and show signs of pleasure when they hear some-one coming, in anticipation of being cuddled and fed. A close physical relation is assurance of being wanted. Children who have been deprived of an opportunity to develop a sense of inclusion, such as may happen in a hospital or series of foster homes where no permanent parental fig-ure is present, often develop shallow personalities typified by apathetic and listless behaviour.

Control

Control is described as the need to establish and maintain a satis-factory relationship with people with respect to power and authority. In this developmental phase, children try to learn how they are able to influence and control some of the things that happen to them. They assert themselves, showing that they are individuals with a mind of their own. This behaviour is typical of the "terrible twos" when children go around "feeling their oats". In this phase the child needs to learn that she is an independent human being who is able to control much of her life, yet one who is dependent on others for many things and is able to

65

use the help and guidance of others in important matters. Through many types of negative behaviour, such as temper tantrums, resistance to toilet training, and frequent use of the word "No", she experiments with this control dimension to see how much influence she can have over her parents and her environment. As she learns to give and take, she works through the extreme alternatives of being compliant or rebellious — she develops *interdependence* rather than dependence or independence. At this stage a child needs an opportunity to make decisions on her own, yet have guidance in doing so. Parental control that is too rigid or dominating robs her of the opportunity to make decisions or exert control and limits her development in this important area.

Intimacy

Intimacy is the need to establish and maintain a satisfactory relationship with people with respect to love and affection — the expression of personal feelings. After a child has developed a sense of belonging or inclusion and worked through his control of this environment, he starts to develop his ability to establish close personal relations based on the open sharing of authentic feelings with his parents and friends. Friendships take on a new meaning as a verbal interchange of feelings and reactions takes place. Developing intimacy is much like the problem of two cold porcupines who want to get close enough to share each other's heat, but not so close as to get pricked by the other's quills.

As we have mentioned, the further development of these areas continues throughout life. The adolescent, for example, is working on these concerns in ways which are quickly recognized. He tries to solve his needs for inclusion by joining several groups. Membership in these groups is most important to him and he will dress and talk differently, participate in activities which hold little interest for him, and resist the opposition of his parents in order to maintain his membership. Pairing with one person in the early teens can also be an attempt to ensure inclusion.

In the control area, the teenager is typically trying to establish a sense of identity — who she is and where she fits into things. She is concerned about what influence she has over things and that this influence on the shape of things is so minute. In daily activities, there is a lot of attention to the rules of the games, especially in sports. Sometimes it is more important to try and work out the rules and their application (was she safe or out) than it is to continue playing the game. Control problems arise frequently in the home and at school, and the rebellious teenager is an example of inadequate management of control concerns.

Intimacy concerns develop in the teens as they experiment with expressions of love and affection with their parents: Am I too big to kiss? To cry? To lose my temper? Later, through the open sharing of hopes and fears, higher levels of intimacy are explored. Finally, the relation between physical attraction and real affection or love becomes of paramount importance for many teenagers. It is common for adolescents to have difficulty expressing their true feelings about life or to have reservations about being open in their relations with others. As the teen moves to adulthood, intimacy expands to a concept of openness — the ability to express feelings and emotions and share one's inner thoughts and feelings with others. True intimacy is based on trust and openness, which are often in short supply in today's world.

Interpersonal Behaviour in Adults

All adults must work out reasonably satisfactory interpersonal relations in the areas of inclusion, control, and intimacy if they are to be happy and functioning fully, using all of their abilities. Now, while all people really desire to be included by others, some have had poor social experiences where they have been snubbed or hurt. Consequently, they may react by withdrawing on the basis that if I don't try to belong, I can't get hurt by being rejected. Or, they overcompensate and attempt to join numerous groups on the assumption that if I try to join lots of groups, some of them will be sure to accept me. Common concerns in the inclusion areas are that I am not interested in other people; that other people aren't interested in me.

In the control area, if a person respects others and has learned the give and take of interdependent behaviour, he tends to be able to share control with others. If he has not learned this give and take or feels insecure with others, he may attempt to dominate all situations through autocratic behaviour in order that what he desires will take place. Through this rigid control of situations, the individual is able to minimize the risk of having to do things which other people may desire. It is a way of maintaining the safe, known situation and preventing the person having to do anything new that might show him up or upset him. The other way to resist control is to insist on individual rights and everyone doing their own thing. Then, without any give and take you won't get in a position to be controlled by others. If it comes to a majority vote, each person is still free to not go along.

The ideal relationships in the intimacy area are close, open, authentic relations with others based on a feeling that other people like me and that I like other people. As we have mentioned, intimacy is similar to the problem of the frigid porcupines: people who have been hurt by getting too close may resist situations where feelings are expected to be shared. They are underpersonal, neither seeking nor accepting close relations, and are nervous about expressing how they really feel about things. As people move toward more open communication with others and can express both positive and negative feelings, they are able to be more spontaneous in their actions and creative in their thinking.

All people cope with their problems in these areas by a variety of procedures and defences which are perfectly normal. As we learn more about ourselves in relation to others and understand better why we do some of the things we do, we should be able to function more adequately in work and family situations. Self-insight also leads to improved social sensitivity which enables us to understand others better and help them achieve more productive and satisfactory relationships. This is one of the major qualities of the successful manager or leader.

WHAT INDIVIDUALS BRING TO NEW GROUP EXPERIENCES

People starting a new group experience bring with them the results of all previous relations with people and usual ways of dealing with needs for inclusion, control, and intimacy. These patterns show up in the attitudes, interests, and behaviour of the new members. In observing member behaviour and trying to understand it, some guidelines for valuable areas to consider may be helpful.

Similarities to Other Groups

New members coming into a group may find things that remind them of previous experiences, especially the people. Other members may remind them of youth with whom they went to school, the teachers who taught them, or workmates from their jobs. The attitudes and feelings they had toward the former person may carry over and shape relations to the new group. This process is often called *transference*, suggesting that people often transfer feelings from one situation or relationship to another. Members are usually partially aware of these resemblances but can be helped to put them into the present by going around the group and saying (or thinking) who each person reminds them of.

Especially important are the transference reactions to the person in authority (teacher, staff worker, coach, manager, or chairperson) as people usually have had very significant reactions to authority figures. Group leaders should be aware that they are the target of both positive and negative feelings from the members through no fault of their own. Some members may also be ambivalent toward the leader and express positive and negative feelings in turn. The important thing is for designated leaders to recognize these reactions, know that they may not have anything to do with them personally, and begin to work out a plan for dealing with them. These similarity reactions explain what many leaders find dismaying in taking on a new group where some members accept them immediately and others reject them.

Members will, in all likelihood, have certain expectations for the designated leader also based on previous experiences. If the leader or other members do not live up to these preconceived expectations, there may be disappointment or anger coupled with aggressive behaviour. The disappointed individual may react by trying to force the designated leader or other member into the expected pattern. Thus leaders who attempt to play a guiding, facilitating role with a new group may find themselves under great pressure to conform to expectations and tell the group what to do.

Attitudes, Beliefs, and Values

Individuals make value judgments about almost every situation. These consistent judgments based on beliefs and feelings are the attitudes that dominate behaviour and lifestyle. A person's attitudes and values develop early in life influenced by their own experiences and their parents, siblings, and relatives. Further developments are influenced by school, peer groups, the media (TV, movies, Internet), and religious activities. In the background, setting many basic parameters of attitudes and beliefs, are the neighbourhood, community, and country. The neighbourhood and country usually have a specific culture that tends to control dress, speech, manners, hierarchical roles, and punishable offences.

While the basic attitudes and values affecting behaviour are pretty much in place by the preteens, adolescence is a time of new activities and physical change that can influence attitudes though most behaviour stays about the same. While we may say "if you aren't a romantic revolutionary in your youth, you have no heart; and a prudent conservative in your senior years, you have no brain", basic behaviour stays the same. This understanding helps us know why youth delinquency retraining, racial prejudice education, and drug addiction treatment have such a disappointing success rate.

Global change has been so rapid for the baby boomer and digital generation that their culture is not the same as their parents' generation and this has created greater dissonance in families, schools, and universities, and many workplaces in the human services. The influx of new conditions from different parts of the world and cultures, pushing toward half of the population in some areas, has added to this dissonance. Realizing that many of our educational, social, and workgroups can have members with different and incompatible values and attitudes helps us seek appropriate accommodations and compromises to manage these contradictions rather than have unachievable goals of changing members' values and resolving conflicts.

Usual Adjustment Techniques

Individuals moving into a group situation become anxious about their inclusion in the group and may feel threatened by the leader or other members. Their response to anxiety will be with a reaction designed to overcome, avoid, or circumvent the threatening situation in order to maintain their equilibrium and comfort. Most defensive reactions can be summarized as either moving toward (fight) or away from (flight) the source of anxiety. A member concerned about inclusion in the group could respond with *fight* by moving into an active role in the group and perhaps competing with the designated leader. *Flight*, or moving away from, could be in the form of withdrawal and underparticipation, or by using the old "foot out the door" approach, saying "I'm not sure I can be in this group, but am trying it out for a couple of sessions." Again this approach of dealing with the problem (threat), rather than the symptom (shyness or aggression), will be most useful in developing a fully functioning group.

Hidden Influences and Agendas

Most people are members of several groups at the same time — family, church, work, and recreation. These groups all have their norms and standards and develop expectations with their members about how they are to behave. It is usual, then, that the members of the groups we are leading will be responding to pressures and expectations from these other groups when they are in our group. Further, if the expectations conflict, a member may be under great pressure to decide which group's expectations to try to meet.

Another similar concept assumes that there are two levels of agendas or goals in a group: ones that are on the surface and ones that are hidden. A member coming late for a meeting explains he missed his bus (surface agenda), but in reality wanted to miss dues collection because he was broke (hidden agenda). A college group member suggests putting on a play to raise money for the graduation dance, while in reality he has just written a play as an English assignment (and got an A on it) and wants the group to put on his play; or a student suggests the class take a break halfway through so members can go outside for a smoke. The hidden agenda is to provide a prayer time opportunity. A group can be working on either agenda or both at the same time. Hidden agendas come to the surface as they are legitimized and encouraged by a climate of trust and acceptance, and groups that were working furiously and getting nowhere start moving ahead.

Testing the Authority Figure

It is important for members to have some sense of the group's status hierarchy for it to function smoothly without a lot of jostling for position, and the most important person to place is the assigned worker or designated leader. Consequently whoever is seen as the authority figure receives a considerable amount of attention and scrutiny. Members want to get to know this potentially powerful person and figure out how she will handle different situations, when she'll step in and clamp down on the group, and what behaviour she will reward and punish. They must figure these things out before they can settle down knowing who's going to do what to whom. The result is a great deal of behaviour and interaction designed to test out the designated leader.

Children approach this testing phase rather openly, often directly asking the worker what she will do if they do such and such. If they are in doubt about the reality of the answer (if they feel, for instance, that it is a bluff) or it is not clear to them, they will go ahead with the act in question to see what happens. Older youth and adolescents tackle the problem a little less directly, often pushing the worker into a corner little by little to see at what point they are stopped. New university students during orientation week may ring the chapel bell for a couple of hours to see if and when anyone comes to stop them. Or, as Dimock's year did, run an obscene flag up the flag pole and anchor it there to test out how the authority figures would handle it. Group members often horse around with one eye on each other and the other eye on the designated leader to note the reaction.

Older youth and adults handle the testing more subtly. For example, university students will ask the teaching assistant assigned to their workgroup how many other groups she has worked with and what happened in them. They ask questions or lead the discussion in such a direction as to find the age, marital status, education, and economic and social position of the leader. They also try to determine why it is this person is working with their group, on what basis she was selected, how much money she is getting, and how much influence the teaching assistant has on their grade.

Experienced workers plan ahead for this testing phase in a group, being ready to show some give-and-take yet establish the group structure and role they want rather clearly. They are also aware that the more upfront and visible they are about who they are and what their attitudes and expectations are, the less will be the need for members to initiate this testing behaviour. If their role does call for a laid-back, facilitator type style they will expect a lot of testing behaviour to be directed to them and not take it personally.

Influencing Groups and Participants

5

The thesis presented in the previous sections of this book suggests that groups are best thought of and worked with as social systems which have structures, norms, and usual ways of doing things. Part Five looks at influencing groups and participants and continues to develop this thesis by assuming that change is most easily accomplished by changing the social system, its norms, and the way it operates. We have looked at how group structures and norms develop and the purposes they serve for the group and individual members; let's now look at how they can be used to influence changes in ways that will increase the productivity of the group and the satisfaction of its members.

New groups establish standards fairly quickly as they move to stabilize their membership and provide structures and expectations about their work. Once the standards are established and found to be useful to the group and its members, they become regularized and are remarkably resistant to change. The standards of the group have been described as property of the group as a whole, or as the group's personality, and are not greatly changed by shifts in group membership. New members influence very minor shifts in norms and it takes several cycles of new members for this shift to become significant unless a "critical mass" of members change over, including most of the previous power structure.

INFLUENCING GROUPS

Group participation is the solvent to unstick the glue of standards. Dimock's study on 31 educational/training programs presented in Part One concluded that growth was facilitated by being actively involved in the planning and decision-making process. Participation in planning maximizes initiative and responsibility among members and becomes a powerful motivator to follow up on the group's agreed upon plans even though they may "rock the boat" on the group's previous standards. These studies and those of a number of others have demonstrated that group participation in planning, encouraging the involvement of all members, is a very effective method of changing group standards. If the entire group makes a decision about a change in standards and member behaviour, it will likely happen. When a group "takes a pledge" together, such as in weight watching or alcoholics anonymous, it is more powerful than when individuals make resolutions for change on their own.

An Attitude Quickly Changed

For 20 years, Dimock was the educational director of the Registered Nurses' Association of Ontario's annual Leadership and Human Relations Training program. It was a 10-day residential program at a resort on Georgian Bay. One year, the participants got very excited about Hula Hoops and wanted to have a contest. These one-metre in diameter rings were swung around the hips and in as much as three or four of the participants were nuns in full dress-skirts to the ground, veiled hoods, and floppy headdress Dimock and several others of the staff thought it would be unfair for them. However, Dimock stuck to his awareness of the usefulness of peer-group planning and encouraged the nurses to go ahead with their planning. All the nuns participated and one of them won the contest. Wow, did Dimock and a lot of others change their minds in a hurry about what fully garbed nuns could do. (Reporting this example and picturing the nuns swinging around with hoops still brings a smile to his face.)

Groups' standards are formed through member interaction and are owned by the total group and can be changed in the same way. Group planning and decision making facilitate the renewed interaction around these standards and are the most effective approaches to influencing change. Once a group starts to review its standards and considers setting new ones, the power of any changes will be increased if the group is functioning well and has strong solidarity.

Early social scientists demonstrated a group planning and decision-making model where they met with a group of workers on a sewing operation and asked them if they would like to set a production goal for themselves. After some discussion it was unanimously agreed to set a goal 10 units higher than what they had been producing. Within five days this goal was exceeded and when the workers met to reconsider it, they set a new, permanent goal that was even higher. After six months they were still producing at that level. Some years later, the same approach was used with a group of workers to change group standards and reduce assembly line blockages.

Similar studies have been made in hospitals where mothers having their first babies were instructed in good nutrition practices. Instituting a group discussion and decision-making approach doubled the number of women using the practices over the previous instructional methods of trying to influence behaviour. Other studies have used the group participation method to pave the way for changing job assignments, introducing new work methods, and assigning some members to a new building.

In the early 1980s the group planning and decision-making model was seen in a very new light as it was the basis of the quality work circle associated with the very successful Japanese management style. Quality work life programs in schools, agencies, and businesses have also made consistent use of the planning and decision-making model to achieve the participation, involvement, and group consensus needed to change group norms. Dimock and Devine's seven-year study on influencing change in community service organizations also incorporated this model under the heading of Systems Improvement Research (Dimock, 1993). In the 1990s, these approaches were revised as Total Quality Management and Strategic Planning. Such studies have increased our understanding of how best to use the participation model focusing on changing the culture or personality to influence groups.

By the end of the first decade of the 21st century, technology improvements and the digital generation of students and employees had started a shift away from these face-to-face meetings. At that time the Internet exceeded television in social influence and hours of use. Many human service organizations are continuing to seek face meetings for the important, high priority planning but the book is wide open on what will emerge with this shift in the digital revolution. Dimock's best guess is that seeing the other people making the decisions with you will remain important as the non-verbal communication can often communicate what is really going on. Computer screens could be enlarged to enable 8 to 12 participants to be viewed at the same time with minor updates in present technology along the lines of the present Skype and messenger programs.

INFLUENCING INDIVIDUALS

The attitudes and behaviour of individuals, especially when they are in a group setting, are influenced by the standards of the group and the other groups to which that individual belongs. Individuals who misbehave in a classroom or in an athletic team can be dealt with directly by the staff person, or an attempt can be made to tighten up the group's standards and pressure to conform, expecting that this will reduce the unwanted behaviour. Our first approach considers discipline a function of the group structure and frequent problems in this area as a symptom of the group not functioning well. The second approach can be the usual one of dealing directly with the individual using whatever power is available to coerce the deviant to abide by rules or procedures.

Regulations which are not supported by the norms of a group or organization usually can't be enforced. The informal practices of the group are stronger than imposed mandates or rules. The official speed limit in Canada is 100 kilometres per hour but the accepted norm is higher. The police in Ontario agree that the real limit is 120 kph and they don't ticket a car unless it's going over that speed. The tax on cigarettes has risen well beyond what is an acceptable norm. Consequently something over a third of all sales are made with underground cigarettes on which the tax has not been paid. While it is possible to try harder to enforce rules that are not supported by the group, such tactics are not usually successful. The more effective approach is to work at changing the norms and usual ways of doing things of the group as a whole.

A Low Visibility Influence of Group Standards

Hedley's leaderless group in a group behaviour course when he was a student at Columbia University included a former major in the WWII German army and two Jews of a similar age. The tension level around the Holocaust issue was high. Dimock had high status in the group, though he was the youngest, since he was the sole member majoring in group psychology and he also was working with groups in a hospital. He was able to model a "don't ask, don't tell" standard to avoid the hot button issue of the Germans' extermination policy of the Jews during the war. If anything close to this issue emerged, he would change the subject. Soon a never verbalized standard was in place.

The group in this example was quite cohesive, and with the support of the other group members, this "don't ask, don't tell" rule was not broken.

Previous sections have presented ways to strengthen groups, facilitate the group's social control, and influence group standards. Other methods of influencing individuals include the following:

Form Groups

The planning and group decision-making model is sufficiently powerful in influence that it works by taking individuals who have no particular relationship with one another, putting them into groups, and encouraging them to consider new attitudes or behaviours. Individuals are more likely to carry out a new approach to something if they are supported in that action by others. Social activist groups, affirmative action programs, religious cults, drug rehabilitation, and youth retraining programs use this approach.

A Forming Groups Example

Many of the groups Hedley worked with over the years were focused on encouraging participants to consider new attitudes and behaviours, but three that quickly come to mind where new behaviour was the primary focus and using group methods was a new approach are the following. A bank president in a speech in Halifax said that his bank was going to assume community responsibility and set up a returning program for the increasing problem of high school dropouts. As the selected educational consultant for the two demonstration projects, Hedley had the participants form groups, which were both learning teams and personal growth groups. These groups increased the participants' enthusiasm for the program and their learning the skills necessary for employment. The outcomes were that all participants got a job placement (but in a branch of the sponsoring bank).

The other two situations using the cohesive growth group approach were the Montreal YMCA fielding its first "family life education" program and John Rennie High School wanting to help students with difficulties. The family life groups did not have a formal evaluation. The participants liked working in the group so much that rather than having lectures and seeing movies, they asked for an advanced group so they could continue. The high school program had an extensive outside evaluation that showed moderate achievement of the program's goals.

Modelling

Observing and identifying with the behaviour of others has an important influence on many people. Research has shown that youth typically model some of the behaviour of their adult leaders and that the quality of leaders' attitudes and behaviour was directly related to the development of the youth in similar areas. A camp study showed that youth who were well accepted by other campers had behaviour that was very "contagious". Efforts by adults to increase their attractiveness to other members typically expands their influence.

Peer Training

Social support for new behaviour is generated by peers taking responsibility for training each other in the new behaviours, rather than bringing in an expert or outsider. Peer training is especially powerful in schools, universities, disadvantaged groups, ethnic groups, and other groups that may have uniqueness that distances them from "outsiders". When combined with using a desirable role model in the form of the peer trainer/coach, a double influence is produced. This understanding has led to self-help groups, networking systems, and community-based development groups.

Providing Information and Utilization Frameworks

Another important tool for shaping behaviour is helping participants develop insights about an experience so they can generalize and apply the learning to another situation. These generalizations provide a utilization framework for experiences. The frequent use of immediate rewards develops conditioning — a specific response to that situation. Only when the response can be understood and applied on a problem solving basis to another situation can it be considered learning. For example, when a child discovers that if he touches a familiar pot-bellied stove he gets burned, he may keep away from it because of the conditioning process of touching and getting burned. Only when he develops an understanding that a variety of receptacles that contain burning materials are also hot and will burn him has he really learned about hot stoves.

It is essential to the growth process that an individual be able to predict the consequences of a variety of possible behaviours in a situation. These predictions are based on insights gleaned through previous experiences and tested against the utilization framework that particular person has developed. Consequently, new information, to be maximally influential, must fit into the already established utilization framework of members or help to modify the frameworks by showing relationships among experiences that will enable participants to more accurately predict the results of future actions.

Experiential Learning

People learn according to what they experience in trying to satisfy their various needs. Providing influential information has impact when it fits into utilization frameworks — a person's usual way of looking at things — or when by developing insights and connections about behaviour and outcomes, it modifies the framework. Experiences that are "learning by doing" oriented are particularly influential in modifying attitudes and behaviour by using both thinking and feeling processes. A group climate of high acceptance facilitates members trying out new behaviour in a "learning by doing" orientation. Immediate feedback describing how a particular behaviour affected the other members helps a person judge the appropriateness of the action. The clearer and more specific the feedback and the more closely it follows the action described, the more influential will be the information.

Dealing with the "here and now" as contrasted with the "then and there" is often used to differentiate experiential learning from other approaches. Thus trying to improve the way members handle conflict may include presenting a new approach, seeing a film of individuals using the approach, and reading about its effectiveness in other situations. To experience experiential learning, the members must try it

79

out in real situations and get feedback on their attempts to implement it. If the members find the approach useful and start to reorganize their utilization frameworks to include it, then getting a lot of support and reinforcement for the new behaviour will help them to follow through with the change. The greatest resistance to influence attempts occurs at the point when the individual has tried it out and is considering incorporating it for keeps.

UNDERSTANDING CULTURAL DIFFERENCES

Over the years, Hedley has typically used two approaches to help him and the groups he was working with understand cultural differences. Every group has its own culture and no two are the same. In business, the salespeople can be the "freewheeling buccaneers" and the office staff "the nit-picking administrators". In a hospital, the operating room culture is very different from the pediatric ward. The differences increase when you go across Canada or to a foreign country. In the same group the differences can be immense: sex and sexual orientation, language, religion, lifestyle, country of birth, and so on, with all the different attitudes, beliefs, and values that go along with them.

When the consulting activity Hedley and his colleagues were to be engaged in had a data collection activity as the start of their work, they would create an internal consultation committee within the community or organization. A major role of this committee or team was to pair with them on interviewing and collecting the data desired and then help them analyze it. Thus, when they went around collecting information about the community or organization (verbal, documents, reports, financial statements), they would go as a pair and both of them would collect the information. When they meet later in pairs and with the whole group of pairs, they would discuss what they had found out and what it meant.

For example, when Hedley and his colleagues started a community development project for the federal Department of Indian Affairs with the Mistassini–Chibougamau Reservation in Quebec, their staff of four used four local members of the tribe as their pairs and interpreters. Hedley did most of the early interviewing and was paired with a young woman from the reservation who was starting university. She would translate the Cree for him and afterwards he would ask about the interview. She'd say things like "I think they were nervous about you as a big shot from the government and a university and just mentioned what they thought you'd want to hear". "So", Hedkey would say. And she would then tell Hedley about their problems in getting food and supplies from the Hudson Bay Store (the only source available) in order that they could leave the reservation and go on their trap line for the winter. They had to agree to send their kids to an Anglican school 900 kilometres away in Ontario to get the supplies they needed. That, of course, was at least as important as the living conditions on the reservation (many families still in tents), which was mentioned in the interview.

In another community development project sponsored by the government in a municipality in Montreal, Hedley had his students, as described above, collaborating on the project. They all had a pair from the planning committee of the YMCA that had originated the project. When the students and Hedley all met together, they would do their business and then have what became "the meeting after the meeting". It had no agenda but became such a rich experience for the Y's committee that they wanted more of the learning-by-doing experiences. Several of these Y groups signed up for our centre's training programs or took a course in their academic program. The process of their work became the content of developing key community leaders.

Rounding out this pairing/partnering method of increasing understanding of cultural differences was to combine it with our research method. Action research is quite unique in that the role of the researcher is to train and facilitate the clients in using appropriate information collecting, analysis, and problem solving methods (the research is done by the clients) to take useful actions on their issue. If there are problems arising from the clashes of different cultures in a group, that becomes the focus of the action research.

As the educational consultant for a three-week residential international community development program for the World Urban Network, Hedley combined these methods. Small discussion/development groups were created using a mix of the various cultures involved. These groups dealt with either clashes around leadership and power, male/female roles, capitalism, socialism, self-help and outside care, and other ethical issues of who was free to do what to whom. As usual the various language groups pleaded to be in the same group but were grateful at the end of the program that this had not happened. (But for a while he was "deadly Hedley".)

81

During the program all participants spent a week in a local community serving organizations in the extremely racially divided city of Chicago. Hedley encouraged all assignments to be designed so that two or three of our participants would go together to the same organization and pair up with a staff person at that organization. This made for three integration experiences (we called them debriefing clinics) — opportunities to consolidate learning without which an internship experience loses most of its educational value. These three were (i) the pair or triad who went together; (ii) that pair and their local partners; and (iii) the 8- to 10-member discussion/development group in our program where that was their agenda for two-and-a-half days.

The second method of understanding cultural differences typically used by Hedley is what he calls "active listening". Early in his career Hedley noticed that when he started his groups with the members introducing themselves, nobody was listening. Everyone was concentrating on what they were going to say. When he moved to pairs interviewing and introducing each other, it didn't help much. But it did remind him of a group technique he'd read about from his counselling days, and active listening became the core of many activities for increasing understanding of personal differences. This core technique is a pause in the activity for participants to demonstrate that they have understood what another person has told them and get feedback on the quality of that understanding.

Following the new group introduction using active listening, everyone would be asked to write down a brief description of what they had learned about the person on the right and left of them and read it to the class. The muttering about that task was hilarious — half the usual group couldn't even remember the names of the two people. Now that members were aware they hadn't listened, they started practising listening and demonstrating an understanding of attitudes and beliefs. The goal was that when we were dealing with an emotional difference in attitudes or appropriate behaviour or practices, we could slow down the argument by requiring each person who wanted to say something to verbalize an understanding of what the last person had said to that person's satisfaction.

Sound easy? Maybe even fun? No way! People resist like crazy having to understand what others are saying about emotional issues. Sometimes the person wanting to speak next would get into an argument about the accuracy of his understanding statements with the last speaker. The class or the facilitator would need to intervene as a referee. This is such a powerful technique that its successes could be outstanding. But for people who can't listen at all when their emotions are high, the whole group can be attacked for having "this silly $\Psi\chi\phi*$ rule".

The training and practice toward this goal would start with safe activities such as participants sharing their personal style of learning inventories, moving on later to sharing attitude and value questionnaires. Regular group decisions about a topic for a group report or study, when to break for coffee and lunch, and assignments to individual members would also be used to check the group's understanding of the rationale for other members' opinions.

A big risk of the effective communication of active listening is that if you fully understood another person's culture and its resulting beliefs and attitudes, you might find that it made sense and you would need to change your cherished beliefs and behaviours. This sometimes resulted in complete rejection of the use of this method.

POWER AND INFLUENCE

Nothing succeeds like having the winning hand. Power and influence are the winning hand — the name of the game. As we have seen there are two ways to get power and influence in a group. One is through the formal or external system that assigns a position and power to give certain rewards or punishments. Rewards may include hiring staff or selecting volunteers, job assignments, office and equipment allocations, disbursement of funds, media contacts, promotion, selecting group members for special activities (playing on an all-star team or attending the mayor's luncheon), or whatever the currency of rewards are in that system.

The other way people may gain power is by increasing their attractiveness to others. This is called prestige power and may be gained by being useful to others; being an attractive person (well groomed, well dressed, an articulate speaker); doing favours for others; or giving recognition, approval, and a lot of personal attention. Some people see the influence process as a banking activity — how much they owe others versus how much they are owed — and are reluctant to use their influence for fear of depleting their account. Studies have shown that as most people gain influence through personal prestige they do use it, and this further enhances their prestige, providing they don't go too far and do something that ignores the group standards. In other words, using power helpfully in an acceptable way gets more power!

AN INTEGRATIVE APPROACH TO EDUCATING AND INFLUENCING INDIVIDUALS

In the 1960s, Hedley established a new department at Concordia University based on these concepts of forming groups, peer training, modelling, experiential learning, and providing information and utilization frameworks. Most of the academic courses worked with the class as a group and had small-group activities or tasks. The learning was experiential wherever practical. Thus the group development courses formed groups and studied them, the community development courses became a community and studied it, the social intervention and research courses went out and did it in the community. Reports showing an understanding of the utilization frameworks related to their hands-on experiences replaced final exams.

A useful example of this integrative approach would be the course in guidance where 25–30 students would form five or six guidance teams. Each team was oriented to course goals of learning some basic guidance skills, going out to a youth group of mid-teens in the community and using those skills, and learning something about themselves in the process. Thus all of the mentioned methods of influencing individuals were in play.

Each team participated in several group-building activities with Hedley as the model facilitator, getting to know each other, exploring a number of elementary interest finders and learning style inventories, using them on themselves, and discussing the results in their team. Then with Hedley again as the facilitating model, the teams assessed how that experience had gone for them and the relevant learnings. The next phase was to role-play sample meetings with their youth groups and practise explaining sample results about the inventories they were going to use.

The cooperating community organizations (YMCAs, Boys and Girls Clubs, etc.) would recruit the teens for the program (never a problem) and provide a room or two for the (usually three) after-school or weekend sessions. Following the project experience, the university students completed the course with a team review of their work as a team, an evaluation of their team project, and a peer assessment within each team to negotiate with Hedley for a course grade.

IN A NUTSHELL

People who meet in groups tend to form standards of operation and behaviour in order to operate more effectively as a group and maintain themselves as a group. Members are expected to conform to these standards and pressure is exerted by the group on individuals to conform to these norms. In this process of social control, a group derives its power to control members who deviate from its solidarity. The more cohesive the group, the more it is able to control its members. Members of cohesive groups who find the group putting pressure on them to abide by group standards may either modify their behaviour or leave the group, depending on their reasons for membership and the attractiveness of the group to them.

While almost all members contribute leadership to the group at one time or another, groups develop a leadership hierarchy and award status in relation to position. This personal status is gained by helping the group be successful and gives the owner considerable influence. Leadership functions either help the group to accomplish its goals or to maintain itself as a group. The most effective mix of tasks and group-building functions depends on a number of situational variables, and diagnosing these variables increases group influence.

The closer an individual comes to demonstrating an acceptance of the norms of the group, the higher will be the social status of the individual. And the higher the social status, the more influence an individual will have on the group.

A group is a social system with structure, norms, and usual ways of doing things. Deliberately planned actions to strengthen or modify that system are a powerful approach to enhancing learning and personal growth, group productivity, and organizational revitalization and change.

The least worst ways of facilitating your learning and that of others and responding to the many concepts and challenges described in this book are the following:

• Help yourself and others recognize the attitudes brought to an experience.

- Motivate yourself and others to learn how to ask better questions about shared experiences.
- Develop these ways of thinking about human behaviour in groups (utilization frameworks), so you and others can make better observations and judgments.

Emerging Understandings of Effective Groups

6

TEAM INVOLVEMENT AND TASK ACCOMPLISHMENT IN OUR DIGITAL AGE: THE GOOD, THE BAD, AND THE UGLY

> "I don't want to go among mad people," said Alice. "Oh, you can't help that," said the cat. "We're all mad here."
>
> — Lewis Carroll

As a faculty member in a graduate school that subscribes to semi-virtual teams to accomplish its program, Raye has begun to notice how the evolution of technology is influencing teamwork and task performance. The following is a first-person narrative of her preliminary observations of her graduate course, followed by the experience of three of her graduate students, some overall dynamics, a summary of lessons learned, and action steps.

This two-year innovative program is taught in an intensive format and is structured in the following way: pre-entry residential interaction lab, followed by year one, which begins with a residential lab course on group process and is then followed by three-day monthly weekends where several courses are covered. Year two starts with another week-long residential lab on learning processes, which is then put into action six weeks later. Following this team intervention, there are several one- to two-day weekends during which students tackle their action thesis project.

Context: Semi-Virtual Teams in a Graduate Program

Students in our graduate program come from across Canada, with a sprinkle from North America, South America, Europe, Asia, and Africa. Approximately 40–50 percent are from outside of Quebec where this university is situated. Professions range from the health and educational sectors, government, social and community services, and public and private organizations. Age range is between 24 and 55 years. This HSI (Human System Intervention) program, with a process consultation, organizational development, and change-agent perspective, relies heavily on teamwork in the form of task groups, consulting teams, coaching teams, project teams, and study teams. In fact, this team perspective is so central to what we do that all our applicants are required to complete an interaction laboratory prior to entry, followed by an initial residential laboratory course in group process intervention. Students move through their program as a cohort, meeting once a month for three days, with the bulk of their teamwork and group support done interdependently through e-mail, Skype, teleconferencing, computer conferencing, electronic voting, doodle polls (polling members ideas, opinions, weightings, and judgments), text messaging, and online databases that provide information and maintain communication.

Sounds great — but is it? Despite all this emphasis on collaborative teamwork and communication technology aimed at facilitating and supporting a team in action, it is not uncommon that, by the time the cohort reaches their studies in the second year, trust is low, individual and group accountability fragile, and commitment to working as a team, while seen as a necessary feature, is not welcomed. Why is this so?

During the second year, by the end of our residential laboratory course on "facilitating individual and group learning processes", students are given six weeks to design a team intervention involving the whole cohort (18–25 students) with an outside, predetermined organization. The team intervention takes the form of a two-day workshop involving approximately 120 participants, all from the same organization. The focus area, which varies from year to year, always has a personally oriented component to it.

Power, Influence, and Trust Issues Emerge

During the lab, as decisions involving design, logistics, and individual responsibility take place, power, influence, and trust issues emerge in spades. Many of these areas are addressed, and work continues at a high pace in an atmosphere of support and challenge. Toward the end of the lab, self-managed design (4) and logistics teams (4) are set up, each working on different facets of the intervention and each having coordinators. Every student is expected to be involved in both design and logistics teams. The eight teams are led by two student leaders (managers), chosen by the cohort and given the responsibility to oversee that the work gets done. The structure calls for interdependence and collaboration between and within teams. Teams are chosen by interest, expertise, and learning needs. The expectation is that when the cohort reconvenes they will be ready to deliver the following day.

The Digital Village

There is no question that this innovative graduate program would not have been possible without the technology that supports it. Many of these graduates experience themselves in a digital village where they are able to access and transmit data quickly without delays imposed by geographic distance. The use of technology is not a problem, for many have not lived in a world without the Internet.

By the end of the lab, students leave excited and empowered by what they have accomplished. They are also anxious and overwhelmed by what still has to be accomplished. The energy is palpable and good will abounds. So far so good!

I have no direct contact with the students during these six weeks. My only contact is with the two student leaders (managers). This is periodic and generally only takes place on request; and if there is no contact, I check in with them to give support and clarify issues that may have arisen. This is usually face-to-face. When it comes time for the student leaders (managers) to oversee the work done by their peers, the fine line between concern and control seems to be blurred. They either feel quite excluded, and keep at a distance, or try to micro-manage every detail. Neither works.

Semi-Virtual Teams Virtually Break Down

Initial focus during the first six weeks following the residential lab experience has usually been on the task. The digital village is abuzz. E-mails fly back and forth, ideas abound, and suggestions are exchanged. The pace is quick and enthusiasm is high. As the work becomes more complex, different individuals push for decisions, others push to keep things open, and still others for more time to do research. Misunderstandings begin to appear, blame begins to spread, and feedback, although sought after, is resisted, ignored, or rejected unless it subscribes to the person's perspective. Conference calls diminish in frequency and when they do take place are often perfunctory, with the usual check-ins eliminated in the service of time.

With the focus solely directed toward the task, communication begins to be dominated by a few members relaying directives of decisions unilaterally made. "Flaming" — a sort of e-mail bashing or "water cooler" syndrome — begins to appear, with individuals starting to talk negatively about their peers. This leads to "bad blood" and, in some cases, open hostility. Subgroups take over, often failing to keep others informed, while still others begin to feel ignored and/or left out.

When the cohort arrives back in Montreal after their six weeks, their state of preparedness is generally poor, their energy level low, and their commitment to key global decisions ranges from compliance to apathy. Specific project tasks have been taken over by a handful of students, with various subgroups digging in or dragging their heels around decisions that were unilaterally made. In addition, overall design of the workshop is disjointed, lacking in adequate flow, and with little to no consideration given to trust building and group development. Content preparation varies greatly from superficial to in-depth with most students relying on "winging it". The experiential activities designed to bring insight and understanding to the various concepts necessary to deliver are often neither practical nor relevant to the population being served. In short, things do not look good.

Lessons Learned

While we have generally managed to work through areas that impact the students' work during the weekend, there are many lessons to be derived from this repeated scenario where a group's productivity, consequently the project productivity, has dropped considerably because of the limitations the group was under.

These graduate students are busy professionals who work hard in their personal, professional, and academic lives. They take their studies seriously and are interested in what they do. They have worked hard during the six weeks with a deep desire to do well and deliver.

Polarity Imbalance: The Tyranny of the "Or"

During the six weeks between the lab and the students' team intervention, as the work becomes more complex and the task focus intensifies, the initial attempt to balance task with maintenance quickly drops to the point of being non-existent. With the continued absence of maintenance, work level begins to drop, interest level begins to wane, and the collective begins to fragment, with the interdependence initially experienced and sought after breaking down. Teams begin to work independently, often at odds with each other, with subgroups within teams isolating themselves even further.

Balance of task and maintenance is difficult at the best of times, but is paramount when team members are working on an interdependent project and living in different geographic places. Understanding that task and maintenance are one unit with polarities that nourish the other rather than opposing forces is difficult, but it is even more difficult to understand and manage in a digital world. Task and maintenance represent opposing but complementary forces in our lives. When the parts are in opposition, energy is not freely available to flow. The complementary is only manifested when the conflict disappears. The challenge is letting go of the tyranny of the "or" and learning how to integrate the poles in order to move forward and create an environment ready for decision-making and supportive actions. In other words, to gain and maintain the benefits of one pole, one must also pursue the benefits of the other and be able to embrace both extremes at the same time, instead of choosing between A and B. Participants must figure out a way to have both A and B and view these polarities as interdependent, something to be managed, not as a problem to be solved (Johnson, 1996).

This coming year, as I work with my grads on a similar project, I have been thinking of specifically setting up assigned GDS Work Teams. These Group Decision Supportive Work Teams would be aimed at reducing some of the technological barriers to collaborative group work, such as unequal consideration of ideas, dominance of individuals, peer pressure, and loss of autonomy. Creating such a supportive monitoring structure may enhance work teams' awareness of personal responsibility toward their colleagues and team members. These GDS Work Teams would be coached in observing for pitfalls inherent in semi-virtual work teams who are under pressure to produce an interdependent project.

Delegation with Trust: Stepping into a Universe of Possibility

The lowering of trust has been a chronic problem in semi-virtual teams that are composed of individuals, subgroups, and/or volunteer teams who are mandated to work on an aspect of a project. The cycle is familiar. A subgroup (person) volunteers to work on a piece of a larger project. Pitfall number one: the mandate is unclear. Pitfall number two: the mandate does not get clarified and the subgroup (person) proceeds to work on the task. They send in their work, e-mails are exchanged, discussion or disagreements ensue, the task is re-assigned or taken over by another subgroup or person, and the work gets redone. There is an atmosphere of discontent and the seeds of resentment begin to grow. Everyone is upset.

The cycle can take on another variation. A subgroup (person) volunteers or is assigned a piece of a larger project. The mandate is clear and the subgroup (person) proceeds to work on the task. They send in their work, they are thanked, and, without their knowing, the task is re-assigned or taken over by another subgroup or person, and the work gets redone. Discontent, resentment, and misunderstandings follow. Everyone is unhappy. When this cycle repeats itself, a state of mistrust gets fostered, involvement lowers, resistance grows; and when volunteers are needed for another task, they are either not forthcoming, or the task gets picked up with reluctance and/or non-compliance. This mistrust–fear cycle constrains and is self-fulfilling. There is preoccupation with boundary-setting and protecting one's turf and the development of protective pairing; collusion and subgrouping begins to emerge. Work gets undertaken with a sense of duty and with little interest or investment.

I have seen this painful cycle in many non-virtual teams. However, the extent to which this occurs in semi-virtual teams is much more frequent. I might add alarmingly so. Once again, I have puzzled about this. As I listen to the power issues experienced, the misunderstandings, and the hostilities that emerge under such circumstances, I am left with the impression that it is easier to dismiss another person's work (in this case a peer) when the encounter and decision taken is not face-to-face.

While Gibb (1972) talks about "learning to trust one's mistrust", he also talks about how the presence of trust provides an environment that nourishes personal growth and unleashes potential, while fear and anger take it away. While no one can program the development of trust in a team, let alone in a semi-virtual team, trusting that what has been delegated will be undertaken with a search for excellence nurtures the development of a supportive atmosphere, and helps to narrow the gap between what is expressed and what is wanted. This is not to say that everything that gets mandated will be done with a view to excellence, but what it does suggest is that trust with delegation paves the way for sharing relevant concerns and allows for data to flow, facilitating healthy decision making and sound choices.

Accountability: A Retreat from Mediocrity

Setting norms that encourage standards of accountability within a team is challenging at the best of times. Instilling accountability as a primary mechanism within semi-virtual teams is even more challenging for non–face-to-face interactions. The person is not in front of you, only the person's work. For many, the easier path is to avoid being transparent and write a perfunctory note of thanks and then stew.

Avoidance or absence of accountability creates resentment among team members who have different standards of performance. Missing deadlines and key deliverables, distributing incomplete work, and/or being unavailable foster deterioration of relationships, encourage mediocrity, and lower commitment. Both the product and the relationship deteriorate.

There is much irony in this vicious cycle. Often team members do not want to call their peers on performance or behaviours for fear this might hurt the individual or jeopardize the relationship. The very thing they want to avoid invariably occurs. The relationship does deteriorate. As lower standards prevail, dysfunctional team behaviour appears and the team begins to stagnate and fails to grow.

The most effective and efficient means of maintaining high standards of performance on a team is peer pressure. When a team holds one another accountable, it establishes respect among team members who are held to the same high standards. It also enables potential problems to be identified by questioning one another's approaches without hesitation.

The Power of the Narrative:
Learning from the Inside Out

The following excerpts are from two of my graduate students illustrating the struggle and appreciation of technology and how this influenced their teamwork. While they were in the same program, they were in different years.

ॐ   Louise

We left our lab on a high. We seemed to have pulled together as a team more so than any of us would have hoped, given the trials and tribulations we had encountered in our group work over the previous year. We had creatively come up with a vision for the workshop we were going to design, and had rallied around the principles that were to guide our work.

However, after having shared a full week of residential experience, we now had to disperse into the outside world, to our full-time jobs and families and find the time to connect with the two subgroups each of us was a part of for the design and logistical preparation of the workshop.

There were three of us in my design team and all lived close by. So we tackled our work through three face-to-face meetings and a few e-mails. My logistics team was larger with six participants spread across four cities. Our meetings were held on Skype and we used e-mail for follow-up.

Our first hurdle was to find an appropriate time for our conference calls. Negotiating one person's commitment on Mondays, another person's unavailability but Monday and Wednesdays, parents in the group wanting to talk after kids went to bed, and one person being in a different time zone left us with Wednesday evenings at nine as the only possible option. This meant 10 p.m. for the person living in the Maritimes. The lateness of the hour was a challenge because calls would start with everyone a bit tired from their days and focused mainly on the call being over in no more than an hour. I believe the time constraints that we accept as a consequence of having a virtual team affect our capacity to appropriately deal with maintenance as we focus on the task at hand.

An additional difficulty of Skype calling, or any teleconferencing for that matter, is the unnatural flow of conversation. People must speak in sequence to be heard; a person trying to interject into someone else's comment is usually not heard by the initial speaker so that everyone else can hear them talking over each other in a confused deaf dialogue. Inevitably as this happens, a third individual chimes in, in an effort to make them aware of the overlap, creating only further confusion. With everyone vying for efficient conversation, this waste of time becomes irritating.

Each week when the hour was up, some people pressed for more time to finalize the decisions being made, while others advocated that we respect our time engagements. In between phone calls and e-mails, Google posts were used so that people could share with the group whatever portions of the work they had been assigned to do. Of course, here again some inefficiencies occurred. Not everyone consulted their e-mails or the posted documents in a timely fashion and the group had to negotiate through more e-mails, whether to wait for them or make decisions and move on. The task-focused people wanted to move on, the maintenance-focused ones wanted all-around inclusion.

In other words, while the technology allows virtual teams to tackle their work, it puts an additional burden on the already complex feat of managing a group's process. It particularly affects the group's ability to attend to maintenance. Not enough time is set aside for this and the context creates additional irritants that polarize the result-driven people from the process-driven people.   ∅

☈   Richard

Since we were all in different locations, it was agreed that we would use telephone conference calls as the means to connect. Planning the effective use of technology and giving structure to it was extremely helpful. Why telephone conference calls? In the first year, a number of us had tried team meetings for different projects using Internet-based programs such as Gizmo and Skype. The experience was less than satisfactory; there was often interference on the line, which seemed to get worse with the number of people on the conference call. A lesson learned here on the use of technology was not to stick with something that was not working.

We then tried a telephone tag system, whereby one person would call another, the other then initiated a three-way call with another, and we were able to connect the four or five team members in this telephone link. The quality was good, and those who made the long distance connections already were on unlimited long distance plans so there was no added cost to any of the participants. This became our means of team meetings. For the most part, it also provided the added capacity of being able to talk by phone and then have our computers with Internet connection up and running at the same time. This meant that during the meeting, we could forward documents to each other and have everyone looking at the relevant documents and providing feedback on the call.

In between telephone conferences, technology also played an important role, as e-mail was used to exchange documents and provide needed written material, instructions, and clarifications.

Although technology became a key tool in our work together, telephone meetings and e-mail exchanges were not enough. The use of technology had its limits in terms of being able to see and feel the big picture. Although the parts each team worked on seemed to make sense, the technology or our use of it did not allow us to get a sense of the flow of the workshop and how each session would feel and fit. We decided to meet face-to-face to see how everybody's work fitted together.

The coming together was an important learning because it did point out some major challenges in the workshop's design and flow that we were able to adjust as a result. We needed to see and feel the design in action. We needed to see and talk to each other about the design face-to-face. People had worked hard on their own pieces and had to go through this process of being together — seeing the design in action and providing feedback for some people to let go of some of the work they had done in service of the client and the team — so that they could recommit to redesign.

Some of the pitfalls of the telephone chain system and similar computer-based telephone conference options is that we were not able to see the verbal cues of the other. This meant providing timely and critical feedback was difficult to some. In one of the teams I was part of, I was having a problem with a member who I felt was not fully committed to our work. This person would never step up and volunteer to take minutes or produce documents and was even absent for one or two of our meetings. I only addressed this when I was face-to-face with the person and by then our team's work had been completed.

As I reflect back on this, I question whether technology can be used as a means by some who are fully committed to go along with the team, but not pull their weight. Technology was an essential tool in our cohort's work together over the six weeks before meeting our client. It enabled us to continue our work and deal with the many facets of putting together a workshop. It alone was not enough, however. We needed face-to-face time to check in and get a feel for the design by actually seeing it and feeling it. Technology, like any tool, can truly help teams do good work together. Knowing the limits of the tool is essential, however, when planning how to use it effectively and efficiently. ⌀

The following narrative takes us on a different journey. The influence of technology is recounted from a consultant's perspective of giving leadership to a "virtual team". This is a powerful narrative that represents a current experience of one of my graduate students who describes his process, his dilemmas, and his insights.

ꝗ   Howard

I'm the change management lead for a program whose main purpose is to align the subsidiaries of a parent company under one global technology system. To manage this work, a central team has been created including representatives from each of the subsidiaries, the parent company, independent consultants, and a team from the supplier of the system. In total, we're around 15 people. My role is to ensure we have a good change management strategy (an external focus) and good inter-team effectiveness (an internal focus). It's this internal focus that has caused a set of unforeseen and interesting challenges during the first few months of the program.

Two workshops were organized so that foundational work on the technical and functional aspects of the multi-projects could be dealt with in a concentrated, face-to-face manner over two short bursts. We also needed to develop a sense of team between the members who worked out of seven different cities and ten time zones. However, because of the great expense of travel and lodgings, I was unable to convince the program director or project manager that there should be significant time devoted to maintenance during the workshops. At the beginning of the second workshop, I approached team building by the group, asking the simple question, "What are the conditions of excellence that we need to establish to work effectively and productively?" This equipped us better to handle difficult conversations, because in each case someone was able to point to the list of seven and inquire into our behaviour. Although the conditions allowed us to manage difficult conversations, they also covered greater schisms that I knew would begin to affect the work once we had all separated again. I left the second workshop satisfied that great work had been accomplished but suspicious that I had propped up the group with surface measures, including my presence, which would no longer be adequate when we were separated.

I was confirmed in my concerns. Once the energy from the action items created during the workshops had dissipated, I began to sense emerging schisms. I say "sense" because most of my intuition was based on silences from one party or another, the tones of e-mails, and passing asides one person might say to me about another. There was no "room" in which I could convene people and see them in action together. I had to expand my concept of the room and begin to listen as someone who is half-blind might. I had no non-verbal clues. I also had few chances to even hear everyone together, so that I could not ask difficult questions of the group with all members present. This led to one-on-one conversations: purported to address issues, I understood this method risked entrenching the issues.

Technology played a part in this. E-mail conversations can drift quite easily into the territory of misunderstanding and emotionality, and for our group they did. Conference calls are disconnected experiences, as the team's local pockets gather in different boardrooms, joined by individuals working from home or another site. On occasions when I took calls from home, I always had the sense of speaking into a hole in the wall, the other side of which was an empty room into which people threw their voices from other randomly placed holes. The sophistication of the phone lines is immensely important — when on phones created for simple person-to-person interchange, the distance can feel immeasurable. When connected by a more sophisticated network, the size of the empty room can reduce dramatically. Even then, listening from a facilitator's stance must be focused and in flow, or opportunities are missed (I missed most of mine).

One old system used by some members in an earlier edition of the central team did not realize a technological glitch that had terrible consequences: no one was aware that when they were speaking, the system was in effect muting everyone else. So if in a heated conversation, one person cut the other off, she could not hear his protests, and if he was to do the same, she would not be heard either; the problem was that no one realized this was a technological issue, and so each person imagined the others were some of the least considerate teammates he or she had ever come across. The consequences in reduction of team effectiveness and trust cannot be overstated.

There are also environmental concerns. Our "virtual" teams are pocketed, in that there are some members who work side-by-side each day. This causes other issues of group incoherence, as subgrouping is predominant and secrets and opinions are shared, and then held by the subgroups. These subgroups can take on the qualities of the environments they work in, and if, as is the case in our project, the cultures of the different organizations are unaligned and sometimes hostile to one another, the issues facing the entire organization begin to manifest in the central team.

So how am I trying to overcome this? First, I've come to maintain that a "virtual" team is a misnomer: this qualifier we use in an almost offhanded way can cause real problems of perception. It is as if we are saying, well, this isn't *really* a team. It's a virtual team. No. It *is* a team, and I suspect the virtual has crept into our vocabulary because it sometimes feels unreal to work hand-in-hand with people across oceans. But it is very real — the needs as well as the feelings — and as soon as we acknowledge this non-virtuality, this essential team, then we can free ourselves from the word "virtual" (unreal) and the limited expectations that accompany it.

I started by calling a maintenance meeting each week between the senior leads. Its purpose, I explained, was to talk about how we were working together. It was difficult to start off, because a central, task-focused project team is not used to pausing to talk. The common assumption was that we are all "professionals" and "reasonable people". There was some muttering about the waste of a whole hour, or that "a half hour would be plenty". Within a few months, the full hour was seen as valuable (I asked). But the group was becoming concerned that we were not including the whole team. I admit to being one of those torn between inclusion and effectiveness. Facilitating a group of 15 over a conference call is a challenge that I believe neither the team nor myself is ready for yet, as I'll explain below

I've also established a 10-question survey that is sent out to the entire team biweekly, asking about 10 areas of team effectiveness. To develop the questions, I used most of the conditions of excellence produced in the workshops and some other crucial areas that the members of the team had voiced as important to the success of the project. I've called a full-team monthly meeting that will present the data and generate action items as to how to strengthen areas seen as weak. Shortly after I sent out the meeting I received one call that said one monthly meeting was not enough.

I sense, though, that one needs to facilitate a long-distance team at a slower pace than a local team. More precisely, I submit that a long-distance team requires longer periods of time in each developmental stage than a localized team. Within project plans, sponsors' expectations, team expectations, the concern over reduced effectiveness because of the vast distances between the team members is never mentioned, as if to argue for corresponding time extensions would question the professionalism and capacity of all of the members. I have a sense that to deny the issue of distance is a way to manage the great anxiety caused by working with strangers that we cannot see, touch, or feel. All trust mechanisms that we have employed since we have formed into groups have been disrupted by our technological capacity. We cannot look each other in the eye. We cannot shake each other's hands. We cannot break bread. We cannot sit quietly in each other's presence. We can only act together, and know ourselves through acting. The technological capacity allows us to know each other only through task. This is half-knowledge, requiring a longer trust-establishment phase. If I move too fast, and treat them as I would any other team, I believe I would encounter great resistance, and perhaps open hostility to the maintenance work.

Some might say, well, so what? Let them confront you and then you'll have a good discussion. Yes, sure, but in a team spread across seven cities, I myself am not attuned enough to "listen" properly to the indications of hostility over such great distances, nor am I certain of how to contain difficult feelings over such great distances. Is it safe to intervene through conference call? Will I know if someone is really upset, if there is real damage happening? My sense is that a more gentle approach is necessary, because the environment is so turbulent, emotionally mute, and task driven, *and the people that work on these projects have chosen this work because of these factors*. It is as if, in a way, the team is used to working with blindfolds on, likes working with blindfolds on, and I have to put a blindfold on myself in order to learn how they speak to one another, how they learn to trust, and only when I can learn truly how they speak, as they themselves are learning, could I propose that we all take our blindfolds off.

I am still in the process of learning about working with a team whose members are spread over long distances. If I can be sure of one thing, it is to be wary of the word "virtual" — there is nothing virtual about any group, any team, and to call it such might cover the real needs, emotions, joys, and conflicts that will emerge, regardless of geography. ✺

Replenishing Our Human Moments:
A Challenge Worth Exploring

Several things stand out for me as I reflect on my observations, the experiences of my graduate students, and the personal narratives that have been written. These logs, as shown in **Figures 10, 11, 12**, capture the experience of many. They help us understand the influence of technology on virtual and semi-virtual teams first-hand.

Technology Is Here to Stay

While technology is here to stay, it is still too early to determine and understand its long-term impact on collaborative work, quality decision-making, and sustained commitment to the task at hand. The importance of understanding this influence cannot be underscored sufficiently. In so doing we would be better able to build interventions

---

FIGURE 10 Common Concerns, Pitfalls, and Difficulties
Experienced in Virtual and Sem-Virtual Teams

1. Support fades when most needed.

2. Teleconferencing creates an unnatural flow of conversation and becomes a disconnected experience.

3. Difficulty negotiating phone calls with different geographic time zones.

4. Focus on big picture lost as teams work on parts.

5. Subgroupings emerge with those working side-by-side.

6. E-mail experience riddled with misunderstandings and emotionality.

7. Trust lowers as technology is allowed to take over.

8. Decision-making structure unclear and not agreed upon.

9. Skills and expertise not used maximally, and in some cases not at all.

10. Mandates are ambiguous and/or unrealistic.

11. Peers not held accountable for deliverables.

12. Technological capacity allows knowing each other only through task.

FIGURE 11 Action Steps When Working in Semi-virtual and Virtual Teams

Suggested Areas	Suggested Action Steps
1. Focus on big picture	• The old adage "It is hard to see the big picture when you are inside the frame" applies here. Sub-teams need to know how their work contributes to the whole and benefits the client system they are serving. • Where possible, decide on a minimum of one face-to-face meeting to get the big picture, understand flow, and physically meet and connect with each other.
2. Set priorities and review them frequently	• This helps navigate your way through setbacks, misdirection, and cynics who set the team's emotional tone.
3. Create a strong feedback and learning loop	• Team members need to regularly reflect on what they should keep, stop doing, and start doing. This needs to be shared with an exchange of feedback for reality testing.
4. Create group-decision work teams	• These GD Work Teams would be aimed at reducing some of the technological barriers to collaborative group work, such as unequal consideration of ideas, dominance of individuals, peer pressure, and loss of autonomy.
5. Hold team members accountable for their work	• Expectations need to be clarified and feedback given with clarity and support. Where necessary, joint problem solving of the issue at hand needs to be done.
6. Celebrate. Celebrate. Celebrate.	• Look for opportunities to celebrate the team's successes milestones that have been covered, and projects that have been completed.

to facilitate the important work that could, should, and will be done by semi-virtual and virtual teams in our future world of today.

FIGURE 12 Teleconferencing Action Steps When Working with Semi-virtual and Virtual Teams

Suggested Areas	Suggested Action Steps
1. Establish maintenance norms	• Set up a prearranged structure that allows for three brief processing periods: (a) Brief check-in as the team starts their conference call (b) Halfway stop and check how peers are experiencing the meeting (c) Closure check-in as to how the team experienced the meeting and what to watch out for the next time In addition, summarize activities to be taken and ensure follow through.
2. Agree-on ground rules	• Team needs to agree and commit to ground rules for making decisions, resolving disagreements, debating issues, etc. Anyone overstepping these ground rules needs to be called on it by team members.
3. Assess and adjust your meeting process	• Where necessary, reset goals and priorities as conditions and demands change.
4. Give opportunity to vent but not blame	• Encourage the team to vent and air their frustrations. However, you need to monitor when it slips into blame, gossip, and gets off tangent.
5. Redirect discussions not involving all team members	• When discussions involve some but not all team members, redirect and encourage those involved to discuss the issue at another time.

What we do know is that the use of technology brings us into a paperless world that is both archival and efficient, permitting meetings without travel. File systems make it possible to re-display information from previous meetings, to revisit old arguments, to show history of a series of arguments, and to resume discussions. My graduate students report that when the text includes graphics and is clear, concise, and consistent in spelling and grammar, and affirming in tone, it has a positive impact, particularly when there is a request, critiquing a piece of someone's else's work or giving a rationale on an action to be taken. They also state that it is experienced negatively when messages are curt and boorish and fail to get their point across to accomplish goals or advances in strategies. Their observations speak volumes and need to be explored further.

As consultants, educators, and coaches in the field of "Human Systems", we have a serious task ahead that may seem paradoxical, but in reality is not: preserving the human touch, whilst celebrating the magnificence of what technology has opened up for us and has in store for us.

EMOTIONAL INTELLIGENCE: THE OTHER SIDE OF BEING SMART

> In the fast lane of business life today, people spend more time on computer keyboards, BlackBerries, and conference calls than they do in face-to-face communication. We're expected to piece together broken conversations, cryptic voice mails, and abbreviated text messages to figure out how to proceed. In this increasingly complex web, **emotional intelligence** is more important than ever before.
>
> — Rajeev Peshawaria, Executive Director
> Goldman Sachs International

What is emotional intelligence (E.Q.)? Why is it getting so much attention these days? What role does it play in the development of effective workgroups? What role does it play in our lives as we become students in our university system, as we enter the workforce, and/or as we give leadership to work teams that need to produce and perform under pressure? Why is it that the intellect cannot work at its best without E.Q.? Why is it that people with high I.Q. often flounder and those with modest E.Q. flourish?

The human body has two brains and two different kinds of intelligence, say scientists: the rational brain and the emotional brain, which control how we think and how we act. Like Siamese twins, the body's brains in the head and the gut are interconnected; when one gets upset, the other does too. The emotional brain can take over the thinking brain and paralyze it when it is feeling anxiety or distress.

These two intelligences are quite different. While I.Q. is important, it is not everything. At best it contributes only 20 percent to the factors that determine life success. Even among talented pools of high I.Q. people, the most valued are those who can cooperate, collaborate, listen, support, empathize with others, and build consensus. It is not that I.Q. skills are irrelevant. On the contrary, they do matter, but mainly as "threshold capabilities" (Goleman, 1998b).

All very well, but what does all this mean? What does emotional intelligence have to do with making workgroups more effective? Why is it so important? Emotional intelligence is crucial for workgroups for it is the essential ingredient that fosters a healthy, productive workgroup environment. An emotionally intelligent group is able to create an environment in which members value their membership, collaboratively focus on what needs to be done, and address issues that need to be dealt with. In short, it has everything to do with sustainability and transferability.

A few words about emotional intelligence: these are "portable skills" that can be acquired by anyone. They develop when we are open to learning and when we are open to feedback from others. They require practice, reflection, and the discipline of noticing. In other words, you have to work for it and be vigilant in its practice for any benefits to be reaped, for it diminishes in impact and value when it gets no outdoor exercise.

Central to emotional intelligence is self-awareness and self-regulation. In other words, emotional intelligence is being aware of one's emotions and knowing how to regulate and manage them. These two sets of competencies are directed both inward toward self and outward toward managing others. They are complex, yet simple. The framework in **Figure 13** captures Daniel Goleman's (1998a) four pillars of emotional intelligence: self-assessment, self-management, social awareness, and relationship management.

Emotional intelligence is the product of two sets of skills: personal and social competence.

In the next few pages, we will examine some of the growing "illiteracy" of emotional intelligence and some factors influencing this trend, with examples of what we see in the university today and its impact on workgroups and the experience and struggle of a very bright person involved in groups, who has woken up to the fact that I.Q. can

105

FIGURE 13 Coleman's Four Pillars of E.Q.

Emotional Intelligence Skill Areas	Emotional Awareness Abilities	Emotional Management Abilities
Personal Competence	Self-Awareness of one's **own** emotions	Self-Management (Self-regulation) of one's own emotions
Social Competence	Social Awareness of **others'** emotions	Relationship Management of **others'** emotions

only "get you so far". Some perceived E.Q. essentials for the development of an effective, healthy group community are identified in an orbiting space station with an international multicultural crew. Concrete action steps for developing and sustaining a team's emotional intelligence will then be discussed.

The New Yardstick of Today

"We're being judged by a new yardstick: not just by how smart we are, or by our training and expertise, but also by how well we handle ourselves and each other" (Goleman, 1998a). We are entering a new era in our world today, where emotional intelligence — the ability to get along with people and make good decisions — is more important to life's success than the academic intelligence measured in I.Q. tests. While an individual's emotional quotient cannot be underscored sufficiently, it is becoming apparent that a groups' E.Q. may be even more important in our world today where most of our work gets done. In fact, it is rare to see an organizational system today that does not rely on teams to accomplish its tasks and produce results. Work in isolation today is relatively rare, while work in relationship to others has become the norm. Teams that learn to function in emotionally intelligent ways remain vital and dynamic in the competitive marketplace of today.

Over the past years, I have been painfully aware that I am faced with an increasing number of students demonstrating emotional ineptitude and struggling with illiteracy about emotional intelligence. This is a remarkable observation as our department places a strong emphasis on areas such as self-awareness, empathy, and interpersonal relations, the importance of teamwork and collaborative decision-making, and the immeasurable value of maximizing team effectiveness and leadership development through the use of field practicums, internships, and facilitation of small groups. While every attempt is made to enhance the effectiveness of work teams, we seem to be producing more dysfunctional teams than our former vibrant, creative, and productive ones. This new trend is disturbing, for it is growing. Why is this so?

Plugged In, But Tuned Out

Technology — cell phones, iPods, BlackBerry cells, laptops, notebooks, online Moodle, online courses, distance learning, video-conference learning, texting, automated phone directory, etc. — used widely with our students today colours much of their social interaction.

Our current culture of efficiency over effectiveness — online course evaluations, search engines used for primary sources, the "just Google" lifestyle mentality, multi-tasking (music + TV + cell) while working on assignments — with language used by students incongruent with university-level standards is driving academic requirements to an all-time low.

We have 24-hour coffee shops where wireless Internet turns night into day, background noise at bars that discourages interaction (cigarette smokers build the real connections due to less noise, fewer people when outside, combined with a commonality), and an increase in people eating out, but with little to no conversation during this activity. We see the rise in boredom in our schools with a decrease of its opposite — engagement and interest — with kids nodding off, or texting their friends, or disappearing into their own thoughts. Age differences that used to be so complementary in the universities, resulting in rich exchange of knowledge and experience, is now not the case. Older students are seen as "odd" by younger students and academic standards have been lowered.

The routine in class these days starts with "please turn off your cells". This leads students to text messaging. They have become very adept at texting without looking at their cell phone keyboard. Now the announcement goes further: "please turn off your cells and no text messaging". This does not work either. The vibrating gadget connected with cell phones allows anyone to know someone has called. A light or flashing light informs the receiver that an e-mail has just come in. Students desperately resort to creative ways of trying to instantly access these messages. Despite feedback, they get caught up in a world of their own, where their self-awareness is dulled and their self-regulation is seemingly non-existent.

This culture of the *now* — where we need it now, quickly, this instant — produces students who send e-mails and expect an answer instantaneously, who display a "why bother with Facebook" attitude when replies on Twitter are so much more immediate, and who do not bother with CDs and DVDs anymore, because a download of iTunes means "I don't have to get off my couch", and so on. As we lose all ability to wait, patience isn't so much a virtue as an annoyance, epitomized by the fact some even text while driving.

The implications of these trends on sustaining and building effective workgroups is enormous. The basis and foundation for good group work seems to have weakened. Building relationships and mutual trust among group members has become increasingly difficult with dialogue harder to maintain and sharing of relevant task concerns more difficult to address. There seems to be little to no interest in engaging in interpersonal understanding and regulating the group's emotions. I have seen teams spend more time interacting with their screens than with each other. They miss cues, tone of voice, rolling of eyes, fidgeting, and non-verbal behaviours that occur. They also miss the impact of their own actions on their teammates. With time, accountability and willingness to take on responsibility seems to be harder to sustain, loyalty suffers, and workgroups, when assigned a task, find it exhausting and difficult to engage in meaningful and interdependent ways where resources and skills are recognized and valued.

With inadequate conditions prevailing and the development of effective task processes not in evidence, it is understandable why workgroups struggle and become dysfunctional, why the quality of the task begins to suffer, and why members experience relief when their work and the group is finally over.

Balancing and Managing Team Emotional Intelligence: The Heart of the Matter

As a university professor in a department of applied human sciences, one of the courses I teach is an undergraduate course in small group behaviour. I have taught this course for a good number of years and have observed the growing illiteracy of team emotional intelligence. The following two episodes, one at the undergraduate level and one at the graduate level, illustrate this growing trend.

Inclusion Turns Out to Be Exclusion: Whatever Happened to Member Needs?

In my undergraduate course on leadership, I use a three-hour teach-in/fishbowl process — a process that involves group presenting and group observing. The process often results in a powerful experience for both the presenting group and those watching the experience unfold.

The Context: During the second term of this undergraduate course on leadership in task groups, the class is divided in symposium teams, each becoming responsible for a central group dynamic focus. Areas typically chosen are decision-making, leadership, power and influence, diversity, and norms. Following their choices, each member is further asked to choose a group dynamic perspective with the aim of exploring and linking it to their team's main symposium focus. These perspectives are drawn from a long list, such as conflict, gender, roles, group development, hidden agendas, E.Q., humour, membership, groupthink, etc. Students are given several weeks to prepare and present their focus and their perspectives to the class in the form of an experiential teach-in. Following their presentation, each presenting group is asked to sit in a "fishbowl", in which I also join. The focus of the "fishbowl" is to understand their process, how they worked together, and how they made decisions. The rest of the class form the outer circle, observe, listen, and halfway through I invite them to share their observations and insights.

The Incident: This particular symposium team had as their main focus "Power and Influence". The team consisted of seven members. Their chosen perspectives were gender, conflict, membership, E.Q., hidden agendas, and group development. Fairly quickly into their presentation, it became evident that there were serious unresolved team issues and that these issues impacted both the quality and product of their work. It was painful to watch.

As the fishbowl progressed, it became evident that there had been very poor inclusion of certain members, to the point of deliberate exclusion, and that destructive norms had been nurtured allowing for no perspective taking, no room for interpersonal understanding or commitment to building the team. There was no effort made to dealing

109

with emotions that were surfacing, which were regularly being suppressed by the more powerful and vocal members who controlled the group's process, and all the while justifying their actions in service of the work that needed to be done.

What became evident was that the topic they were studying and presenting to the class had only impacted them intellectually. Their actions bore no relation to their words. The group's emotional intelligence seemed shaky. Their ability or desire to regulate and work with their group's emotions was missing. More stunning was the absence of group awareness of the emotional havoc that was being sewn as the group went about preparing for their task. When I ventured to ask the member who had studied membership and had presented his section with great skill whether he saw a relationship between his perspective and the inclusion and the subsequent development of membership in his group, he drew a blank and genuinely seemed puzzled by the question.

This is not an isolated experience. More and more groups seem disconnected with their group's process and lost in the emotional dynamics that surface. In some cases, there is self-awareness and poor self-regulation; in others, there is no group self-awareness and no self-regulation; and in most groups, there seems to be a lack of structure that allows effective task processes to emerge.

Espoused Theory versus Theory in Use: Now You See It, Now You Don't

In a graduate course I recently taught, students spent time studying, designing, planning, and eventually implementing a workshop on emotional intelligence to an outside organization. They were a very bright group of professionals, skilled in their field, experienced in working on project teams and task groups, and knew their data.

The Context: It became evident, as I worked with them and as I watched them work with the outside system, that they had developed counter-productive norms of self-regulating as a team. While they stressed the importance of a group's emotional intelligence to their clients, and the vital importance of handling a group's emotional level, they ironically did the reverse of what they espoused. I noted that they tended to suppress expressions of discontent and frustration arising between peers unless it was directed toward authority figures. They had developed ways of smoothing things over, unwittingly nourishing an environment that lacked safety and freedom of expression, and an environment in which feedback was limited and issues that needed to be dealt with were ignored, or brushed aside. They had difficulty balancing support with confrontation, and the fine line between concern and control often was blurred. When interpersonal or group issues surfaced with occasional outbursts of anger, they were either greeted with silence and "business as usual" or members withdrawing and pouting. On the surface, the group seemed competent, open, and focused.

Choice to Wear Blinders: Before working with the client, the cohort was challenged to focus and study their own emotional intelligence. It became clear that while they had skills to address this as a topic on an intellectual basis, they had difficulty looking at it on a more personal basis. Their resistance was such that subgroups in most cases became non-functional, and groups that moved forward were the ones that had remained open to learning from the inside-out. Their willingness to go further facilitated the development of processes dealing with task, team, and individual needs. In short, they had attended to the inescapable influence of their team's emotional underworld.

As mentioned earlier, this was a bright and hard-working group. However, their unwillingness to examine their own emotional intelligence disabled their capacity to establish norms of supportive behaviour. They chose to wear blinders, resulting in groupthink with no proactive engagement in problem solving when confronted with critical issues and with no appreciation of the necessity for collaborative decision-making (Janis, 1972). When difficulties arose, they blamed circumstances or those in authority. When the course ended, the group's termination level was determined by the social networks it had formed. While termination took place, closure did not. Their choices influenced their product, contributing to their lack of understanding of the value of dealing with their group's emotional intelligence.

The Inner Rudder: Our Most Precious Resource

The following is a poignant narrative of a very special, intellectually talented individual who continues to struggle with her self-regulation. Her self-awareness does not serve as an inner rudder for her choices, thus influencing negatively her focus and her energy. I have included this narrative (with her permission) as her profile represents gifted individuals whose talent and intellect, while an asset to a group, are a challenge to access and, ultimately, a challenge to the group's productivity and effectiveness.

⚡ Katie

My experience as a member of groups has been quite varied, running the gamut from project groups to teaching teams. When I look back at these experiences and reflect on my role as a member, one aspect stands out: the impact of my personal emotional intelligence. The ups and downs of my ability to recognize my E.Q. have had a profound effect on my role in these groups, as well as on my personal development.

Throughout my university career, I have been privileged to work with inspiring individuals. My interaction with these individuals over the years has put into perspective the low level of E.Q. I have possessed. As a student and colleague, I strove to portray the image of a self-confident, outgoing individual. It has not been easy to recognize (after self-reflection) how lacking I am in the self-regulation, self-awareness, and motivation areas. I aim to present myself as someone who is in control of herself and her emotions, when the reality is I fluctuated greatly during the last five years. Working in groups has helped me to be able to realize my areas of development within E.Q. While it has not been an easy journey, it has been one that I feel has benefited me greatly.

My self-regulation is shaky at best. While I felt that I was successful in monitoring my reactions to situations when working in groups, the reality is that I was hiding from my emotions, not regulating them. The results of this were quite dramatic. After having portrayed myself as someone who was appropriate in her reactions, I eventually would break down crying, confusing my fellow group members and rendering myself unable to function in a group setting. My experience as a student in a pivotal third-year experiential learning course was particularly devastating, as the second semester saw my performance spiral down, resulting in a lowered performance and grade. My fellow group members were also quite angered by my actions, which not only impacted their grade but also highlighted my inability to be a true member of the group, as I had put on a "fake" face to them and my professor. While it could be said that I maintained my social skills and empathy, the reality is that these attributes were as false as the persona I presented. My empathy was too pronounced, and I made promises and comments in order to deflect the attention from my crumbling sense of self and performance capacities.

As I reflect upon this event, it also is very telling of my level of self-awareness. Although I received feedback from numerous members of my group, I refused to examine what had happened, and why it had occurred. When asked to become part of the teaching team the following year, I eagerly accepted, hoping to prove that I was in fact a "good" team member. Once again I maintained the facade. This seemed to fool no one but myself, and I suffered another breakdown at the end of this group experience. I once again refused to acknowledge what was really going on, and continued. This lack of self-awareness resulted in a new personal low, as I struggled to keep up and accomplish the tasks I had volunteered for. I evaded and outright ignored the concerns of my fellow group members, insisting that I "was fine". My motivation also reached a new low, as I was too busy keeping up appearances to fully enjoy and engage in the work that the team was doing. It wasn't until a very special member of the group cornered me and gave me much needed feedback. Unlike previous attempts, this normally mild-mannered individual refused to back down until I acknowledged what I was doing to myself and the group. This once again resulted in a new low for me: I was not motivated to change my actions, and my lack of self-awareness crippled me, as I was unable to self-regulate. I attempted to become more self-aware, but quickly shielded myself from the pain this self-awareness caused and once more reverted to my old ways.

This pattern continued until new members joined the teaching team and I had a heart-to-heart with the professor on the team. I credit her strength (as well as that of my team members) in being able to deliver feedback in a way that hit close to home, as well as helping me to see the impact I have on the group when I refuse to examine my behaviours and their underlying emotions. The literature will tell you that self-awareness is key to strong emotional intelligence. It saddens me to realize that while I may one day have a higher level of self-awareness, it will not be enough. While I can become aware of what I do (and do not do), the reality is that I rarely put this self-awareness into action. Instead, I tend to once again revert back to my script and attempt to hide my sufferings. I have held teams back due to my choices and will continue to do so until I take action. While I still struggle with highs and lows, the very fact that I can write this personal narrative is heartening, as it gives me an indication of how far my self-awareness and, consequently, all areas of my E.Q. have improved. I know my areas of development, as well as the script I follow when I have hit a low. While the change is not complete, I am making the effort to stabilize and continue my upwards movement. I have a long way to go, but I am determined to continue my journey toward a stronger Emotional Intelligence. ☝

The following takes us on a different journey where we catch a glimpse of the emotionally laden working environment that cosmonauts and astronauts face as they experience life in space and/or life in long-term simulations. While the following illustrations are not necessarily indicative of all teams in space and/or simulations, it is indicative of how complicated living and working in an orbiting space station can be. It is also indicative of the importance of developing and using the "portable skills" of emotional intelligence in work teams whether on earth, in extreme isolation, or in space.

Essentials in an Orbiting Space Station: Choosing the Right Stuff

What is often neglected in the busy schedule of training crew for flight is the preparation of the crew to work and interact together as a group, and to work and live effectively under difficult circumstances. Emphasis is on technical procedures and use of equipment for performing experiments with little to no consideration of human factors.

The demanding paradoxes of an astronaut are quite challenging. Patricia Santy (1994) in her ground-breaking book, *Choosing the Right Stuff*, describes their professional demands this way: "They must be sure of themselves, but not too sure; they must be competent but not arrogant; they must love to fly, but appropriately fear flying; they must be confident about their abilities, but not grandiose; they must react quickly to danger, but not be impulsive; and they must obey authority, yet be independent". How many mortals could stand up to these seemingly endless injunctions? Santy (1994) observes that the "delicate balance of these paradoxical expectations results in an internal tension experienced by every pilot and astronaut."

Living in an Orbital Space Station

Stress Factors

Stress factors encountered in space are numerous: keeping up with the timeline, getting the work done without errors, fear of failure, redoing an experiment gone wrong, repairing equipment that is broken, housekeeping, sleeping, hygiene practices, taking orders from ground control, being continually watched and assessed, orbital weightlessness, confined and cramped conditions, leisure time, primitive comforts, little privacy, isolation from earth with no quick and easy way to return, monotony, fatigue, missing family and loved ones, etc.

Getting along with Crew Members

When you combine paradoxical expectations and the numerous stress factors encountered on a daily basis, one can understand the difficult and unusual circumstances astronauts operate under. Getting along with fellow teammates can become an acute problem under such circumstances. Self-management (self-regulation of one's own emotions) and relationship management of others' emotions begin to be key. Reported anecdotes drawn from diaries of cosmonauts during the MIR Station era illustrate these interpersonal tensions and difficulties. Two cosmonauts in space for 211 days hardly spoke together. One is reported to have written, "Humming to myself, I float through the station. Is it possible that someday I'll be back on earth among my loved ones and everything will be alright?"

In another incident, one of the psychologists reported that a cosmonaut cried out to ground control: "Fetch me back quickly, I can't work any longer with these zombies." Another cosmonaut, who had been in space several times, wrote in his diary, "What conditions are necessary to provoke the committing of murder?", and answering his own question when he said referring to the MIR Station, "Barricade two men for two months in a 7-metre long capsule." In yet another situation, an experienced cosmonaut wrote, "The hardest thing during a flight is keeping relations with ground control and among the crew. With growing fatigue there is danger of lapses."

Background and Context

During 1999–2000, I was principal investigator of a set of space mission experiments conducted in Russia called SFINCSS (*Simulation of Flight of International Crew on Space Station*). Twelve subjects were recruited for this space isolation simulation. Three groups of four were isolated over a span of 240 days: one crew (4 male Russians) over the whole period; the second crew (3 Russians and one East German); and the third crew (an international crew of 3 males and 1 female, with the males from Russia, Japan, and Austria, while the female was a French Canadian) for 110 days each, one entering upon exit of the other. Thus, there were simultaneously functioning groups at any given time, similar in structure to the International Space Station (ISS) flight (Kass & Kass, 2000; 2001).

115

Prior to the space simulation, team-building sessions were carried out with each of the crew. The original plan had been for a comprehensive team training within each crew and jointly between the three crews, but trying to pin down the promised time schedule was not possible. In addition, at no time were the investigators able to have all participants present at any given time, as different tests were being scheduled simultaneously. This reduced time with incomplete crew, coupled with the fact that there were never joint sessions with the three crews, compromised the work we (my co-investigator Dr. James Kass and myself) had hoped to accomplish in the area of emotional intelligence, where skill training and feedback would have taken place. The original project involved specialized group-interaction training that would equip the crew to deal with problems arising from teamwork and work relations.

Critical Incidents During the Space Simulation
There were several critical incidents that occurred during the space simulation that caused misunderstandings and conflicts:

- Frustration erupting into a fist fight over one crew member's expressed jealousy of another crew member's ability to speak English

- The New Year's Eve kiss leaving the female crew member feeling violated and vulnerable

- The closing of the hatch between the Russian crew and the international crew following the fist fight and kiss, influencing planned joint team talk-sessions

- A crew member abruptly deciding to leave the experiment and exit the isolation chambers because of all the frustration he was experiencing

- The Commander of the international crew who did not speak Russian and had to give a daily report to the Mission Control who only spoke Russian, resulting in his needing to depend on his Russian crew member to translate for him

These critical incidents were not dealt with constructively. The various emotions that were bubbling over were either suppressed or misplaced, influencing the various crews' emotional underworld. Their lack of problem solving skills, ability to give each other constructive feedback, and emotional support contributed to poor relationship management skills between and within the crews. This, coupled with their lack of built-in team norms that would have given the teams a platform to weather the storm, was sadly lacking. There were many lessons to be learned from this situation, not the least of which being the importance of building a foundation for a team's development of emotional intelligence.

A Summary of the Significance of E.Q.

My experiences during the 1994 Canadian CAPSULS mission, the 1999–2000 Russian SFINCSS mission, and the USA research training project with NASA Ames Research Center all point to the same five essentials for the development of an effective, healthy group community in an orbiting space station:

- Getting along with crew members
- Sensitivity to self and others

FIGURE 14 Pointers, Highlights, and Key Features for an Effective Healthy Group

1. Teams operate on two levels: work and emotional.

2. Technology today colours most of our social interaction, shifting the basis and foundation of norm development within work teams.

3. Quality of teamwork suffers when members lack emotional intelligence.

4. Collective emotional intelligence is complicated, as a team needs to attend to both the relationship management of its members and the group as a whole.

5. Team self-awareness does not automatically lead to team self-regulation.

6. Team suppression of discontent and frustration is counter to healthy team self-regulation.

7. Perspective-taking nourishes the building of team emotional intelligence.

8. Structures that allow emotional dialogue to surface also increase participation and collaboration among members.

9. Team performance increases when members recognize and acknowledge the emotions that surface and influence their work.

10. Team relationship management paves the way for healthy group communication with other workgroups within and outside of the organization.

FIGURE 15 Norms That Foster Individual and Team Awareness and Regulation of Emotions

Areas to Invest in	Action Steps
Interpersonal understanding and perspective taking	• Take time to understand a perspective that represents the opposite of your own. • Check your understanding before stating your own. When you do so, share how you are feeling. • Respect differences in perspective. • Periodically ask quiet members what they are thinking. • Check for understanding and commitment of decisions being considered. • Acknowledge your disagreement with issues being discussed. • Acknowledge your observations, if you sense unresolved undertones.
Affirm, acknowledge, and reach out	• Acknowledge contributions, work efforts, and thoughtful interventions of others. • Where possible build on teammates' ideas, suggestions, and comments. • Acknowledge feedback, even if you disagree with it. • Acknowledge moments of caring. • Provide emotional support, where needed. • Listen, listen, listen.
Create a trusting and safe environment	• Take time to include new members and bring them up to speed. • Exercise your discernment, integrity, and moral compass. • Allow for conflict to surface. • Acknowledge differences and misunderstandings. • Admit your mistakes and move on. • Avoid blaming, shaming, and/or gossiping about absent members. • Focus on problem solving, not blaming.
Surface team members' skills, hidden talents, and resources	• Take time to understand the range of expertise in the group and, where possible, affirm and maximize these resources.

Continued next page

FIGURE 15 (continued)

Areas to Invest in	Action Steps
Surface team members' skills, hidden talents and resources (continued)	• Acknowledge when you can't comprehend what is going on or when you feel inadequate to the task. • Follow through with commitments and responsibilities you have chosen to take on or that has been delegated to you. • Do not say "yes" to doing something when you want to say "no", or when you have no intention of doing it. • Ask for help when you need it.
Transfer-in	• Start meetings with a transfer-in. This means checking in with each person as to how he or she is doing. This needs to be done regularly. This does not need to take much time, but enough time needs to be given so that each person feels heard. • Listen and take into account what is being shared because it may colour the emotional tone and energy in the meeting. • Do not turn a transfer-in into a personal problem solving session.
Mid-process check	• Regularly structure a mid-process check-in giving members an opportunity to state their observations and feelings of how the meeting is progressing. • Listen to what is being said and redirect the process or direction, where necessary.
Transfer-out	• End each meeting with a check-out. This is very important as this will give members a sense of how each member experienced the group's productivity. • This will also help members understand the group's level of task involvement and emotional investment.

• Interpersonal awareness
• Functioning as an interdependent group over a long period
• Developing effective problem solving skills

Except for the last essential, the other four represent self-awareness and self-regulation of team emotions. Ironically, these are the same essentials as on earth.

> The Whole Image of a Man in America today is: "You can't feel."
>
> I say, "God damn it, let me feel."
>
> — A Vietnam veteran

Teams are cauldrons of bubbling emotions. Anyone who has worked in a team noted the inescapable influence of a group's emotional underworld. Anyone who has been a member of a task group experienced the swing in shifts in the work level of a group when the emotional level of the group had not been taken care of (Kass, 2008). On an average, we experience 27 emotions each waking hour. With nearly 17 waking hours in a day, we are likely to experience throughout the day about 459 emotional experiences. If one does the math, more than 3,200 emotions guide us through the week, and more than 170,000 each year. These are astonishing numbers and underscore the importance of building and nurturing a team's emotional intelligence, particularly as most of these emotions will occur during working hours.

DIVERSITY IS A FACT — AND A VALUE

> A shoe factory sends two marketing scouts to a region of Africa to study the prospects for expanding business.
>
> One sends back a telegram saying: *"Situation is hopeless stop no one wears shoes".*
>
> The other writes back triumphantly: *"Glorious business opportunity stop they have no shoes".*
>
> — Author unknown

This story of two marketing scouts represents our story: the same situation elicits different responses, one that captures our hopelessness and the other our hopefulness. The evolving story of diversity as seen and experienced today is both challenging and difficult. Newspapers are filled with eye-catching headlines: "Tolerating the intolerant" (*Montreal Gazette*, March 28, 2010); "We're not all the same" (*Montreal Gazette*, March 14, 2010); "City's face changing rapidly" (*Montreal Gazette*, March 10, 2010); "Niqab heats up rights controversy" (*Montreal Gazette*, March 3, 2010); and so on. While we cannot escape what is happening, we do know we can change our response to what is happening. We can, like the second scout, say, "Glorious opportunity — diversity is our new reality."

While our classrooms, offices, and factories are becoming a "rainbow coalition" of people from many different cultures, socio-economic backgrounds, and races, we are still in our infancy in managing, let alone unleashing, the potential that diversity has in store for us.

Today 54 percent of Canadian immigrants belong to a visible minority that will rise to 71 percent in 2031 with at least one Canadian in four being foreign born — the highest level since Confederation.

Already, the people we call "minorities" are a numerical majority across the world. By the year 2056, we are told the "average" United States resident will list his/her ancestry as African, Asian, Hispanic, or Arab — not white European. In many city school systems, Caucasian students are already a minority in numbers. It simply is a fact — one for which many of us are ill-prepared.

Diversity surrounds us. Our cultural tapestry shows in the things we eat, the tools we use, and the words we speak:

> Think about our daily routine. A typical Canadian/American citizen awakens in a bed (an invention from the Near East). After dressing in clothes (often designed in Italy), he/she eats breakfast on plates (made in China), eats a banana (grown in Honduras), and brews coffee (shipped from Nicaragua). And after breakfast, he/she reads the newspaper (printed by a process invented in Germany and on paper originally made in China). Then, flips on a tape recorder (made in Japan) and listens to music (possibly performed by a band from Cuba). (Ellis, 1998)

When one reads this, one could not help but chuckle ...... so true ...... so delightfully true, and yes — this does represent diversity.

"Walk the Line": A Glimpse into How Diversity Is Experienced Today

Over the past 10 years, the topic of diversity has always been covered at the beginning of my undergraduate course in Leadership in Small Groups. Due to a growing diverse student composition, I have felt that it was important to highlight the impact diversity has in small groups, whether working in one or leading diverse teams. In addition, it needed to be conveyed that they should not leave their ethnicity at the door. To this end, our initial session has habitually included some form of an exercise that allows the students to visually see the diversity of the class. While the experiential learning activity has remained the same, this year saw a new activity emerge, as the teaching team I was working with saw the need to create something that more dynamically illustrated the impact of diversity in workgroups.

The original exercise comprised students placing various coloured dots on a large map of the world, indicating the following information:

- Where they were born (red dots)
- Where their parents were born (blue dots)
- Where their grandparents were born (yellow dots)

Students were then asked to share their origins, as well as those of their parents and grandparents, with emphasis being placed on the cultural diversity of their family groups. A teaching team member would then record this information, and the class would be asked for their observations of the data shared. Students were then divided into groups of five to six persons to discuss the following question: "Given your experience and background, how does your cultural origin influence your participation in groups?"

The small group discussions that followed were quite animated with students showing high involvement and interest in this activity. The data that was subsequently shared with the class pointed to how national culture influences our values and how values influence our attitudes, which in turn influence our behaviour. This powerful data helped students gain insights into how easily judgments are made based on observable behaviour, with little appreciation or understanding of why these differences exist. In addition, what surfaced was the realization that while we may come from the same cultural background, we should not leap to the conclusion that everyone in the same culture is the "same".

While this exercise did illustrate the diversity of the class, the teaching team felt (after critiquing the exercise) that the impact of diversity being experienced today, with its current broadened definition, was not effectively being highlighted. While students would see where their peers came from, and while dialogue brought out more information, it did not truly capture how diverse these students were.

After discussion, it was proposed that a more dynamic process be created to replace the (perhaps) more static one. The teach team felt that earlier exercises addressed diversity that was obvious and that while acknowledging and addressing those differences is important, it was also necessary to bring to the surface other differences that we may not have readily recognized but experienced. Eventually what emerged was an activity entitled "Walk the Line". This activity consisted of students standing in a line, each facing the same direction. Questions around diversity were asked, and the students would, accordingly, either step *forward* or *backward* depending on their situation surrounding that question. The questions were as follows:

1. If you have a grandparent who was born in Canada, take one step forward. If you have a grandparent born outside of Canada, take one step backward.

2. If you have parent who was born in Canada, take one step forward. If you have parent who was born outside of Canada, take one step backward.

3. If you were born in Canada, take one step forward. If you were born outside of Canada, take one step backward.

4. If you are an only child, take one step forward. If you have any siblings, take one step backward.

5. If you have a post-graduate degree, take three steps forward. If you have an undergraduate degree, take two steps forward. If you have a CEGEP degree, take one step forward.

6. If you speak more than three languages, take three steps forward. If you speak two languages, take two steps forward.

7. If you are tall (5'7" and taller), take one step forward. If you are short (5'6.9" and down), take one step backward.

8. If you consider yourself to be below average weight, take one step forward. If you consider yourself to be above average weight, take one step backward.

9. If you are heterosexual, take one step forward. If you identify with any other sexual orientation, take one step backward.

10. If you are male, take one step forward. If you are female, take one step backward.

11. If you are Caucasian, take one step forward. If you are First Nations, take three steps backward. If you belong to any other visible minority, take one step backward.

12. If this exercise had an impact on you, take one step forward.

These questions were designed to create a visual and emotional impact. The types of questions, as well as the marked difference in the direction of the steps, contributed to this. Students did not openly express their reaction to certain questions nor the direction the questions required them to take, but many seemed uneasy. At the end of the exercise, students were standing at various distances in the classroom. They were then asked to share their feelings about where they had ended up versus the "original" line they had all stood at. This activity increases in impact the higher the numbers and the larger the physical space, as it allows for a greater range of variations from the original line and, in so doing, dramatizes the differences.

The Diversity Configuration That Emerged

At the front of the class, Ross, one of the students, stated his lack of surprise at where he was located (at the very front). As a tall, white male, he said that while he had not expected to be all the way at the front, he did not feel uncomfortable with his final position. One male student, however, expressed that while he was in the front of the class, he felt as though he was there not because of what he had done, but what his parents and grandparents had accomplished and experienced. This statement was particularly interesting as this student visually did not represent the "norm" of the average white male (he had dreadlocks, large piercings, and numerous tattoos). His statement of not feeling as though his position in the classroom was justified was echoed by many students.

Most of the students in the front did not express surprise, but some did express discomfort at how far they were from their friends and peers. Similarly, the students at the back of the classroom expressed frustration that their accomplishments were not reflected in their positioning, and that their cultural backgrounds should not indicate how "far back" they should be in relation to the others. The teaching assistant for the course was at the back of the class and expressed her feelings on her position as one of frustration and resignation. She explained that although she was a successful individual with a university degree and a coordinator's position at her place of work, she knew that based on her skin colour (she was black) she would always be at the back. However, she continued to say that while society may place her at the back, she knew that she was really at the front of the line.

While it was made clear that these questions were merely one method of analyzing diversity, many students seemed affected by the results. The emotions that were raised were very different from those we had seen when using the previous activity: the impact of the diversity was not only visual, but also raised disturbing questions. The size of steps students took seemed to vary according to the direction required to take and question being asked. Advancing steps seemed larger than those that put individuals "farther back". Was this due to the fear of being judged or judging others? Were students honest when answering, or did fear and other emotions hold them back?

The impact of this exercise on the teaching team was clear. When critiquing the session, it was apparent that the activity created drama and visual impact. The statements made further highlighted the emotions the exercise brought forth. The impact on the students was seen and heard through the discussion it created, although the silence of many students might be more telling. This activity gave the community a chance to be aware of the diversity in our class, both hidden and explicit. The questions challenged us to look at how we label others (fat/thin, tall/short, their sexuality, level of education, etc.).

While many discussions usually focus on the physical and explicit aspects of diversity, it is important to also address those aspects that may not be as easy to categorize. Asking the students to reflect on the range of diversity in the class helped them recognize that how they see others in the classroom also affects how they see others beyond the classroom — task groups in their work places, the community they live in, and the places they travel to. It also helped them see that while individuals may personally perceive themselves at the front of the line, where they may end up, based on the perception of their peers, may be entirely different.

This activity allowed our students the opportunity to examine how they view themselves and others, as well as how they may be perceived by outside forces. While the process may not have been easy, it continued to impact the class over the year. Eventually, some students came to appreciate and recognize that while diversity brings challenges, the possibility of acquiring different skill sets and resources, when combined, can create new knowledge and ideas, resulting in a workgroup that is more creative in its product.

Personal Thoughts

My experience as a faculty member teaching about groups and leadership has taught me a few sobering lessons about the subtle, inherent dynamics of diversity in groups. What I have noticed is that when teams are formed on a spontaneous, voluntary, or involuntary basis, diversity issues play a subtle role: how a student is welcomed into a group that is already formed, how a group member is listened to, how a group member's ideas are given attention to, or even how a group member is given feedback. While there are a myriad of other dynamics underlying these responses, such as personality differences and willingness or ability to take on responsibility, unspoken elements of diversity (age, sex, status, culture, socio-economic background, education, etc.) play a role in influencing a team's cohesiveness, trust, flexibility, and/or capacity to leverage its resources and skills.

Personal Narrative about Diversity

Delia, who is the teaching assistant in my undergraduate course in Leadership and Small Groups, is also a graduate student in our Human System Intervention Program. In her own words she drew us into her world of pain and personal growth as she reflected on her journey as a member of one of the graduate teams. Her focus became "the world in me" and not "me in the world"

✎ Delia: A Member's Perspective

When I think of diversity, my mind peruses words such as "tolerance", "acceptance", and "accommodation". As a result I can't escape the fact that I wonder "Who are you to tolerate me?" The dichotomies, good/bad, superior/inferior, inclusion/exclusion, are all a part of the vocabulary we use to discuss issues of diversity. As a Black, English-speaking, female growing up in Montreal ...... diversity is something that I have been aware of and have had to deal with for my whole life.

Currently completing my Master's Degree in Human System Intervention, what astounds me most is the level of intolerance for anything that strays from the mainstream. The idea of thinking outside of the box is squashed and not seen as an asset but as a hindrance. What saddens me most about all of it is the fact that I myself have remained quiet and allowed this assembly-line sameness to dictate the climate of our group.

I am overwhelmed at the fact that, as a result, we have limited ourselves in the vast richness of our collective. Many an opportunity to share what could in fact be "the idea" has been lost because the message was not delivered in a fashion "suitable" to the majority. The language of tolerance and acceptance has guided our journey together. What would our experience as a group be if words like "celebrated" and "partnerships" were our guiding light?

I can recall one such place where diversity was embraced and the best of everyone was capitalized upon to create something quite magical. It is a place called Kinkora. Kinkora is a summer camp where people of all ages, races, cultures, languages, socio-economic status, and health status come together to celebrate their uniqueness and capture the best of one another in an effort to learn, explore, and understand one another. The minute you pass the gates that separate Kinkora from the tolerating world, something happens. People see you for all you are, they don't tell you that they have forgotten about the part that makes you distinct. They embrace you for the good, the bad, and the ugly. They ask about what they don't understand to better understand you, not to use it against you in an effort to keep you down.

I have been a part of camp in one form or another for the past 16 years, and there is a reason I keep coming back. Camp helped me understand that I don't have to be a stereotype in order to be noticed in the world. It was a message of hope and faith. Hope for my future, open to being anything I set my mind on, and faith that I had (and continue to have) the capacity to make it happen. It was not about being black or female; it was about identifying the strengths I had as a person. These strengths were acquired because I am Black and because I am female. These qualities have shaped my understanding of the world. What has shaped yours?

A wonderful friend of mine from camp once said to me many years ago, "Go where you're celebrated, not where you are tolerated." Corey, you have no idea how many times in my life I have heard those words in my head, and they have given me the strength to separate myself from situations that were breaking my spirit. Thank you.

After she wrote about her experience of membership and diversity, she agreed to write about her current experience of diversity as a coordinator of a program that gives leadership to troubled teens.

Delia: A Facilitator's Perspective

I always thought I really understood the concept of diversity. That is until I realized that I was looking at diversity from my own perspective and not that of the "other". I have thought myself to be a rather open-minded individual, but I have had the opportunity over the last few years to recognize that I have much room to grow in this area of my life.

As a facilitator, I have enjoyed the challenge that diversity has brought into my work. I have at times struggled with managing the space between what the adolescents want and what their parents desire. It is in this space that I have learned the most. It has not been about everyone being heard but about everyone listening. It is the same for me. It is when I truly listen and do not attempt to get my point across that I grow as a worker.

I remember when I had a client who was questioning his sexuality. He had a lot of fear about telling his parents. When speaking to the parents and trying to assess how open they would be to discussing their son's sexuality, I had the experience of being very angry about the things that they were saying. In my head I wondered what kind of person would turn their back on their own child simply because of who they chose as a partner. Upon reflection, I started to put myself in the parent's shoes. They were dealing with the hopes and dreams that they had cultivated for so many years about what they thought their son would grow up to be. It was not that I agreed with what they said, it was that I was able to put myself in a place where I was able to probe them to understand why they were saying what they said. I was not defending my own "openness" but genuinely exploring their perspective.   ∅

Diversity is a strange and wonderful creature. It pushes us as facilitators but most importantly as people. It is in this push that we create many diversified ideations that allow for rich discovery. The hidden element of diversity is when we, as facilitators, fool ourselves into believing that it is not present. When we do this, we deny the many colours of the rainbow.

Making Differences Matter

These past three years I have been a consultant to a profit-making organization that places a high value on learning and personal growth among its workers. I was originally called in to help facilitate dialogue between plant and office managers. The owners had a high respect for their managers, recognizing their hard work and loyalty. When I first met the managers I was struck by the wide range of diversity I was confronted with. This group of 12 persons represented a rich array of diversity: multi-discipline, multinational, multi-racial, multilingual, multi-educational, and multi-religious. They came from different backgrounds: Russian, Portuguese, American, Jamaican, Indian, Guyanese, Polish, Chinese, and Jewish. They had different religions: Unitarian, Sikh, Orthodox Christian, Hindu, Anglican, Catholic, and Jewish. Their education ranged from high school to master's degree. There was diversity at every level. What a group — a real powerhouse.

Over the three years, I set up self-directed interdependent project groups that were mutually beneficial to both the plant and the office. They set their focus, their team composition, meeting times, and their criteria for success. Trust and respect for each other developed, coaching teams voluntarily emerged, and results were celebrated. They took initiative to "green-light" open discussions. It was powerful.

The success was influenced by several things: the organization's leaders, in this case the owners, had worked hard to define "belonging" in terms of a set of values and a clear sense of purpose. They had worked hard to fully tap the human resource potential of every member of their management workforce, managing disparate talents to achieve common goals. They had also managed to transcend what organizational leaders fear most from diversity — the lowering of standards and a sense that "anything goes". They had managed through hard work (trial and error), clear vision, and openness to develop a genuine workplace of diversity:

- They understood that a diverse workforce needs to embody different perspectives, opinions, and insights.
- They had created an organizational culture of high standards of performance.
- They had a well-articulated and widely understood mission.
- They were able to create a culture where their workers felt valued and respected.
- They delegated, listened, and understood differences.
- They had created a culture that encourages personal growth and development.
- They began to see the need for open discussion and trust between different departments and had set things in motion for this to happen.

Prior to the last management retreat, one of the owners met with four representatives of the management team to ask them for feedback about the previous retreat and input about the upcoming retreat. Their feedback and input indicated their trust in the process and their belief that their feedback would be heard. Their desired focus for the retreat was "leadership and communication". Their feedback to me was, "a less crowded schedule" and more time to "network". They got both.

Space Agency/Space Station. Diversity in Action: A Rare View Behind the Scenes

Diversity in An International (Space) Organization[1]

The European Space Agency (ESA) is a good example of international cooperation, being an organization of collaboration whose origin is even older than that of the European Union. There are now 18 member countries, with a number of additional countries when including the army of resident contractors at the various branches of the Agency.

Teams are typically very international in nature. There can be as many countries represented as members of a team. The common language most often used by a team to communicate with one another, English, may not be the mother tongue of a single team member. Two Italians will speak together in English so that the French team member can understand. Despite this diversity, the teams generally function very well — the cultural origin of a team member being quite unimportant.

There are a number of key ingredients that help the teams to function well:

1. Common working language: fluency in English (written, spoken, and reading) is required for working at the Agency. Moreover, common spaceflight jargon is used.

2. High-level education: All team members are university graduates, often with two or more degrees of higher education behind them.

3. Common basic interest: those joining the Agency usually have a deep interest in all things to do with space flight.

4. Similar economic standing: members of staff (and resident contractors) earn good salaries (above that of local professionals or civil servants with similar education).

5. Similar consequences for failure or mistakes.

6. Diversity of cultural background is common to all — all staff feel like expatriates, even those few locals, who are a small minority in the very international atmosphere.

---

[1] Dr. James Kass, physicist, who works at the European Space Centre, contributed to the following section. His observations cast a useful framework for the management of diversity under certain types of circumstances in an international environment.

These basic ingredients, more often than not common to all members of a team, ensure that members of teams working on any particular project, despite coming from quite diverse professional backgrounds and nationalities, feel like they make up a homogeneous entity. They have considerably more in common with one another than with other members of their own cultural group outside the Agency, their friends from home, or even their family members.

It is often said that cultural diversity brings rich and different approaches to solving problems and can thus enrich a group. This is probably true. At any rate, coming from different countries, different disciplines, and different organizations, team members certainly can bring a rich diversity to ideas and ways of working to a group.

Of course, as with all seemingly ideal pictures, there are always downsides: some of the ingredients listed are not quite commonly shared in a healthy manner; some employees are indeed "more equal than others", e.g., permanent staff have job security, possibilities for professional advancement; and some special privileges, which temporary contractors (making up almost half the staff at the Agency) do not share. Moreover, a fairly rigid and pronounced hierarchal structure can contribute to lack of openness and diminished freedom to speak one's mind, when the division or section head is too strong-headed. These factors can diminish the quality of the key ingredients listed above and result in de-motivation and diminished quality of work.

Nevertheless, all told, professional and cultural diversity at the Agency can and does provide a healthy atmosphere and good teamwork provided that there are sufficient key ingredients shared in common.

In the next section, James Kass, who was acquainted with all the parties cited below and having worked closely with most of them in his capacity of training them to perform experiments in space, writes the following about his observations about diversity in space.

℞ James Kass: Diversity in Orbital Space Flight
Although members of the teams building the rockets, preparing the scientific payloads, and those in the ground-operations teams can go home to their families in the evenings or at least after some days' work, this is not the case for the teams working and living together and isolated in orbit around the Earth (or the Moon) — or, in the future, on a journey to Mars.

Some of these orbital teams have been quite diverse, culturally and professionally, in Soviet/Russians-led missions, NASA-led missions, and, finally, on the International Space Station (ISS). It is rather more difficult to assess the quality of a space team's functioning because there is little documented information; this is especially sensitive with an international team and/or culturally diverse team members. Anecdotal information, however, always exists, and this can certainly be drawn on.

The Soviets often flew non-Russian Eastern Block citizens on their flights, as well as some other countries' citizens; but an interesting period began when NASA paid the Russians a goodly sum for flying American astronauts on the MIR (Russian) space station. The relationship was sensitive because, in principle, rather than an equal collaboration, one organization (NASA) was paying the other for a service. Most of the time this was quite successful with few hitches related to the diverse crew and their customer-service provider relationship.

There were some exceptions, one of which has been well-documented and is worth noting here. Jerry Linenger, an American astronaut on the MIR station, was an example of a crew member who behaved in a manner that underlined some sensitive ingredients that were key, but not quite commonly shared. He was the customer, and he proudly and stubbornly carried out his job as a good American astronaut should without much respect or adaptation to the working and living culture of the Russian cosmonauts on the MIR station. When a leak occurred on the station causing a problem with ventilation and the crew were advised to stop exercising, Linenger refused to cooperate: the Americans were paying the Russians for a service, and the latter should deliver and he (Linenger) needed exercise to keep healthy. For the Russian crew (Tsibliyev and Lazutkin), who were working hard trying to mend the leak, this was not understandable and certainly was not an example of a team holding together. Linenger did not have much confidence in his Russian team members and was critical about their handling of the difficult situation, both while in orbit and after the mission. Here was a relationship of un-equals — the customer and the service provider; this need not have been a problem, but under pressure, and with some difficult characters, the ingredient of inequality of members of the team can certainly lead to problems.

A very different example occurred during a visit to the MIR station by a German astronaut, Reinhold Ewald, who was present when a minor fire occurred. He ingratiated himself with his Russian team members (also Tsibliyev and Lazutkin), staying with them during the difficult event, and even later after the mission, refusing to say anything detrimental about his colleagues.

Another key ingredient that was different for each crew was the consequence of failure: for the Russian team members, mistakes made could tally against their end-of-mission bonus, which was of great importance for the well-being of their families for years to come; the consequences for the "international" crew were rather milder. Different consequences for different team members can certainly affect behaviour and stress very differently, which can (but need not) lead to a lack of cohesion and common goals.

Another example of a key ingredient that was different for each crew was the living accommodation at Star City, where the crew trained and lived. The Russian, European, and American crew lived there, but there were major differences in the comforts of life. Whereas the Russians lived in cramped, standard, simple apartments, the Americans stood out in that they had large and comfortable American-style houses purposely built for them so they could "feel at home". This certainly did not contribute positively toward team spirit; instead it underlined the economic and cultural differences of the team members. It may be noted that the European astronauts' living quarters (in the "Profilactorium") were not much more comfortable than that of their Russian colleagues.

On a positive note, the new era of the ISS has certainly launched a period of healthier Russian–American collaboration. Teams of three are usually alternately headed by an American or by a Russian, both contributing toward transport and building of the commonly used station. In principle, this certainly works toward a healthier atmosphere of teamwork. ✇

In looking over these "Diversity in Action" examples, I was reminded of a possible implication for leveraging diversity, namely screening and selecting team candidates on the basis of their competence in handling diversity along with other professional criteria. When I showed the international company the "Making Differences Matter" example, one of the owners reported that this competence in utilizing diversity was so important that staff who couldn't do it were let go.

FIGURE 16 Best Working Conditions for Diversity

1. Common working language.
2. A clear set of commonalities among group members.
3. Relevant expertise in the workgroup membership.
4. Common basic interest.
5. Shared goals and values.
6. Similar education.
7. A well-articulated vision/mission by the organization.
8. A desire to be part of the organization and play a role in various team projects.

Another possible implication of the examples is making diversity-oriented team building and training a required component for any program created or proposed for an organization's use or sponsorship. This would provide an opportunity during a program's trial period to assess its ability to establish the eight best conditions recommended in **Figure 16**.

Bibliography

Bass, Bernard M. 1990. *Bass and Stogdill's Handbook of Leadership*, 3rd Edition. New York: Free Press.

————. 1985. *Leadership and Performance Beyond Expectations*. New York: Free Press.

Burrough, Bryan. 1998. *Dragonfly: An Epic Adventure of Survival in Outer Space*. Boston: Harper Collins.

————. 2001. *Clear Leadership*. Palo Alto, CA: Davies-Black.

Cartwright, Dorwin, & Zander, Alvin (eds.). 1968. *Group Dynamics*, 3rd Edition. New York: Harper Collins.

Dimock, Hedley G. 2004. *Outcome-based Program Development and Evolution*. Concord, ON: Captus Press.

————. 1993. *Intervention and Empowerment: Helping Organizations to Change*. North York: Captus Press.

Ellis, Dave. 1998. *Becoming a Master Student*. New York: Houghton Mifflin Company.

Fiedler, Fred. 1987. *New Approaches to Effective Leadership*. New York: Wiley.

————. 1967. *Theory of Leadership Effectiveness*. New York: McGraw-Hill.

Fiedler, Fred, & Chemers, Martin. 1984. *Improving Leadership Effectiveness*. New York: Wiley.

————. 1974. *Leadership and Effective Management*. Glenview, Ill.: Scott, Foresman.

Goleman, D. 2006. *Social Intelligence*. New York: Bantam Books.

Goleman, D. 1998a. *Working with Emotional Intelligence*. New York: Bantam Dell.

Goleman, D. 1998b. What makes a leader? *Harvard Business Review*, Nov–Dec.

Hare, A. Paul. 1976. *Handbook of Small Group Research*, 2nd Edition. New York: Free Press.

Helgesen, Sally. 1990. *The Female Advantage: Women's Ways of Leadership*. New York: Bantam-Doubleday.

Hersey, P., Blanchard, K., & Johnson, D.E. (2007). *Management of Organizational Behaviour: Leading Human Resources*. Englewood Cliffs, NJ: Prentice-Hall.

Janis, Irving. 1972. *Victims of Groupthink: A Psychological Study of Foreign-Policy Decisions and Fiascoes*. Boston, MA: Houghton.

Johnson, Barry. 1996. *Polarity Management: Identifying and Managing Unsolvable Problems*. 2nd edition. Human Resource Development Press.

Kass, Raye. 2008. *Theories of Small Group Development*, 4th Edition. Montreal: Concordia University, Centre for Human Relations and Community Studies.

Kass, Raye, & Kass, J. 2001a. Teamwork — Work During Long Duration Isolation. 52nd International Astronautical Congress. October 1–5, Toulouse, France.

———. 2001b. Psychological Training for Small Groups. *Medico-biological and Psychological Studies in the Experiment with Extended Isolation*. International Conference, Russian Academy of Medical Sciences, June 5–6, Moscow, Russia.

———. 2001c. Teamwork During Long-Term Isolation: SFINCSS Experiment GP-006. In *Simulation of Extended Isolation: Advances and Problems*. Institute of Biomedical Problems, Moscow, Russia, (2001), 124–47.

———. 1994. Understanding small group behaviour with a view to maximizing team effectiveness and task accomplishment. In *CAPSULS, a 7 day space mission simulation*. Final report and scientific results (Sponsored by the Canadian Space Agency), held on January 20–27, 1994, at the Defense and Civil Institute of Environmental Medicine. Toronto, Ontario.

Kass, Raye, Kass, J., Binder, H., & Kraft, N. (2010). Conflict handling modes of three crews during a 264-day Space Flight Simulation. *Journal of Aviation, Space, and Environmental Medicine*, 81(5), 502–505.

Lencioni, Patrick. 2002. *The Five Dysfunctions of a Team*. San Francisco: Jossey-Bass.

Mintzberg, Henry. 1980. *The Nature of Managerial Work*. New York: Harper & Row.

Napier, Rodney, & Gershenfeld, Matti. 1989. *Groups: Theory and Experience*, 4th Edition. Boston: Houghton Mifflin.

Santy, P. 1994. *Choosing the Right Stuff*. Westport, CT: Praeger Publishers.

Zander, Alvin. 1982. *Making Groups Effective*. San Francisco: Jossey-Bass.